Art Today and Every Day:
Classroom Activities
for the Elementary School Year

Art Today and Every Day:

Classroom Activities for the Elementary School Year

Jenean Romberg
and
Miriam Easton Rutz

Parker Publishing Company, Inc.   West Nyack, N. Y.

© 1972, by

PARKER PUBLISHING COMPANY, INC.
West Nyack, New York

Library of Congress
Catalog Card Number: 70-175197

PRINTED IN THE UNITED STATES OF AMERICA
ISBN—0-13-049056-3
B & P

To Our Mothers, who encouraged us.

A Word from the Authors

Have you ever wanted an art lesson that won't take a lot of time, a lot of preparation, and a lot of clean up, but will be fun to do and also be a learning experience? As Art Specialists and traveling art teachers for the Elementary grades we set out to solve this problem for teachers with and without formal art experience and background. Art is a vital and enriching part of the life of every child and should be a part of every day. It can be done with a minimum of "mess" and be a pleasant, successful, enriching, daily experience for all involved. The ideas for *Art Today and Every Day* were conceived, gathered and put together as a book to meet these needs.

This book is full of ideas and projects for every season, every holiday and for those days when art will brighten up the day. The projects are relatively simple, carefully planned to fit within the time limitations of classroom teaching, adaptable to any elementary grade level and can be successful no matter what the experience or background of the teacher or child. There are no complicated, hard-to-find materials. All that is needed — apart from the simple materials — is lots of enthusiasm. The projects are all fun to make and something a child will be proud to hang in the classroom and carry home.

Each monthly section includes ideas for holidays and seasons as well as those that provide experience with various media and techniques. The format is simple. An illustration appears on the upper right-hand corner of each page so that the idea can be easily seen when "thumbing through" for an idea. By surveying the page briefly you can see how the project is done. All materials needed for each activity are listed on the upper left-hand side of the page. The simple step-by-step instructions are illustrated to make the explanation clearer. As an additional aid for the teacher, common "pitfalls to avoid" are covered at the end of certain projects.

We hope the days will be filled with endless possibilities for making art exciting when you use *Art Today and Every Day*. By making art a part of each day, children will be exposed to new ideas, various media and techniques and happily motivated to further exciting creative experiences and exploration in art. They will discover new ways to express their own ideas, experiences and feelings.

We would like to thank all those teachers who so freely exchanged ideas with us, enabling us to share with others through the publication of this book. Our special appreciation is extended to family, friends and co-workers who have encouraged us while we were preparing the manuscript. We hope *Art Today and Every Day* will make art an exciting, enriching and happy experience for children and teachers alike.

Jenean Romberg
Miriam Easton Rutz

Table of Contents

October   continued

November   65

November   continued

December   93

January   121

January   *continued*

February   143

April   continued

May   217

May   continued

June   243

Art Today and Every Day:
Classroom Activities
for the Elementary School Year

September

19

LINE MOVEMENT

Materials:
1. two colors of construction paper, 9″x12″
2. glue or paste
3. scissors
4. pencil
5. paper punch
6. yarn

Steps:
1. Draw a moving line diagonally across one sheet of construction paper.

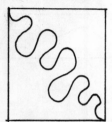 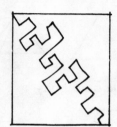 

2. Cut carefully on the line.
3. Glue one half of the design on the whole sheet of paper. Glue the other half on the other side of the paper.

4. Punch a hole in the center top.
5. String yarn through the hole and tie. (This way both sides of the design can be seen)

BIRD TREE

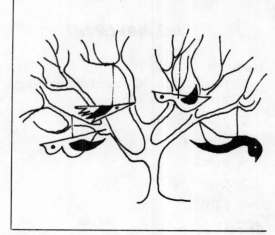

Materials:

1. construction paper (scraps, bits and pieces)
2. glue or paste
3. scissors
4. string or thread and needle
5. dried branch or piece of tumbleweed

Steps:

1. Fold paper and cut out the body of the bird. (any size)

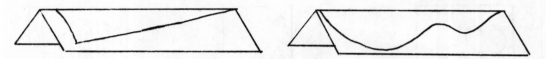

2. Cut out wings and tails. Glue onto body.

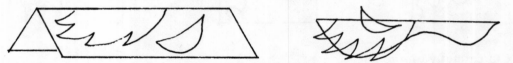

3. Use crayons, pencils, ink or felt pens to add eyes and beaks. (You can decorate as elaborately as you wish)

4. Sew the thread through the back of the bird and tie to the branch.

Variations:

1. Make birds of all the same size or of all different sizes.
2. Make the birds all in shades of one color or in a variety of colors.
3. Do one large bird tree by setting a very large branch in a bucket of sand or dirt. This would make a very nice library center piece.

VEGETABLE and/or FRUIT PRINTING

Materials:

1. Vegetables and fruit that can be cut to reveal a pattern inside: green peppers, cucumbers, apples, oranges, onion, cabbage, etc.
2. thick tempera paint
3. paint brush
4. paper to print on

Steps:

1. Cut vegetables and fruits in half. Some can be cut into more pieces.

   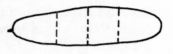

2. Paint the tempera onto the surface of the fruit with the paint brush.

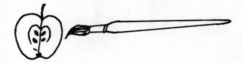

3. Stamp the vegetable or fruit painted surface onto the paper gently. Lift straight up and stamp again. You can get 3 or 4 printings each time you paint the surface.

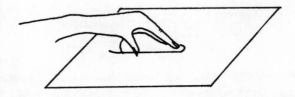

Hints:

1. Let the children pass their stamps around for a variety of prints on their paper.
2. Use only one color on each vegetable or fruit unless it is washed before using on second color.
3. Some suggestions for paper: newspaper (ad sections), manilla, rough grain, colored construction or tissue paper.

TISSUE CITIES

Materials:
1. 5"x5" square of light blue tissue paper
2. (3) 5"x5" squares of different colored tissue paper
3. scissors and black crayon
4. soft bristle brush
5. starch—liquid, in small containers
6. 9"x12" white construction paper

Steps:
1. Tear the light blue tissue paper into pieces.

2. Put a little starch on the white construction paper and put a piece of blue tissue down. Paint starch over it. Continue this until the paper is covered and pieces are overlapping. This will make the sky.

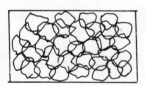

3. Cut the colored squares of tissue into all different sizes of squares, rectangles, triangles, and circles. Put them together to make houses and buildings.

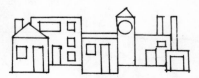

4. Put them over the background on the construction paper. The paper will still be wet from the starch so lay down the city pieces and put starch over them. You must be careful when putting starch over the city so that the color of the tissue does not run.

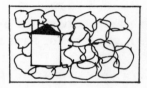

5. The following day you can put on details and outline the buildings with a crayon if you want.

SPACE PICTURES

Materials:

1. 12"x18" white construction paper
2. crayons
3. thin black tempera paint
4. wide paint brush

Steps:

1. Have child draw a space picture. Suggest the use of stars, flames from rockets, moon, people on the moon, spaceships, sun, etc. (See suggested samples)

2. Remind children to color very heavily with the crayon. This does not mean so much pressing heavily as it does going over the drawing with the crayon several times. Also, some areas should be solid color.

3. Paint over the picture with the very thin, runny black paint to make the scene look like it is in outer space.

Hints:

1. The paint should be thick enough to turn the paper black but thin enough to run off the crayoned parts.
2. Set up a table for painting the black wash, covered with newspaper and set up for three or four people to paint at one time.

PAPER BUILDING

Materials:

1. 9"x12" or 12"x18" construction paper
2. construction paper strips of various widths: 1"x12", 1½"x12", ½"x12", ¼"x12", in complimentary colors
3. paste and scissors

Steps:

1. Lay the large sheet of construction paper on the desk. Arrange various strips on the paper to make a flat background design. (Discuss plaids, horizontal and vertical designs: discourage putting Xs on the paper.) When you have a suitable or pleasing design, paste all of the strips down.

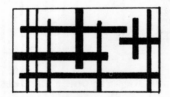 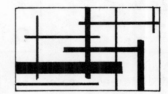

2. Show the children various ways to curl, fold and bend strips of paper. Demonstrate how to attach to the flat paper. Then let them go. They will come up with marvelous creations.

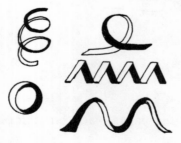 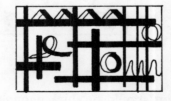

5 DOT ACTION PEOPLE

Materials:

1. a piece of newspaper, classified section, cut to 12″x18″ or 9″x12″
2. tissue paper, any three colors
3. liquid starch in a small container
4. wide paint brush, at least 1″
5. black crayon

Steps:

1. Tear the tissue paper into medium size pieces.
2. Paint the newspaper with liquid starch and lay on pieces of tissue paper. As you put down each piece of tissue paper cover it with a coat of starch. Remind the children that they don't need to cover every bit of the newspaper and encourage them to overlap the tissue pieces.

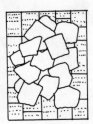

3. Let dry thoroughly. (As this takes awhile, you might wish to make this a two day project)
4. Using the black crayon, make five dots on the paper far apart. Then make stick figures running, jumping, skipping, sliding, etc. At one dot draw the head. Draw hands and feet at the other dots. Then connect with lines for the body. Don't forget elbows and knees.

Hints:

1. Have the children practice drawing the people while they wait for the paper to dry.
2. Several figures might be drawn on the paper.

CRAYON AND FINGERPAINT

Materials:

1. two pieces of white paper, same size (construction or butcher paper)
2. crayons in bright colors (scraps of crayons are best)
3. brown tempera paint mixed with liquid starch
4. paper for mounting

Steps:

1. Coat one piece of the white paper with several colors of crayon. Color heavy strips of varying widths.

2. Place the colored paper on newspaper. Apply a coat of the brown fingerpaint on top of the crayon surface. Fingerpaint a design, making sure the crayon shows through.

3. Then place the other piece of white paper on top of the fingerpainting and rub gently with hand. Carefully pull off the top paper. You will have the original and a one-color print.

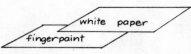

4. When dry, mount on one piece of paper, next to each other.

Hints:

1. It will not take more than about two teaspoons of fingerpaint.
2. Remind children to fingerpaint with one hand only.
3. After fingerpainting, move paper to a clean paper so that the newspaper doesn't stick to the white paper.

WATERCOLOR SUNSETS WITH SILHOUETTES

Materials: Step 1

1. 9"x12" white construction paper
2. set of watercolors
3. soft bristle paint brush
4. small piece of sponge
5. container of water

Materials: Step 2

1. black construction paper
2. glue and scissors

Steps: Part 1

1. Lay the white paper on the desk and completely wet the surface of the front and back with the sponge. The paper should be very wet yet have no puddles.

2. Choose sunset colors (red, orange, yellow, purple) and paint one strip at a time across the paper. Because the paper is wet the colors will run together and blend. Make some strips thicker than others.

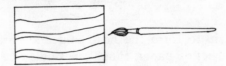

Steps: Part 2

1. Draw a silhouette on black construction paper. Suggestions: sailboats, buildings, trees, animals, birds, people, etc.

2. Cut out a ground or water strip from the black construction paper, 12" long. Glue it on the watercolor sunset.

3. Cut out the silhouettes and glue to the ground line.

ROLLED PAPER ANIMALS

Materials:

1. 4½"x6" colored construction paper
2. (3)—3"x10" strips of construction paper (for dog)
3. scissors
4. paste or glue

Steps:

1. Take one of the 3"x10" strips of construction paper and cut the ends to look like dog paws.

2. Glue this onto the colored construction paper, 4½"x6", so it arches up. Make both paws go forward.

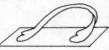

3. Roll one 3"x10" strip to form the head and add ears, nose, eyes, mouth, etc., with scraps of construction paper. Pinch one side of the roll to make the nose stick out.

4. Cut one 3"x10" strip in the shape of a tail.

5. Attach head and tail to the body arch, using glue.

Hints:

1. Try making other animals, using the 4½"x6" piece of paper as the base and any number of strips to construct the parts of the animal you are making.

HANGER PEOPLE

Materials:

1. a wire hanger
2. a nylon stocking
3. scraps of all colors of construction paper for facial features and other decorations
4. scissors and glue or paste

Steps:

1. Holding the top of the hanger with one hand, pull the bottom of the hanger with the other hand to make a diamond shape.

2. Pull the nylon stocking over the hanger and tie it at each end with string. Cut away the extra nylon.

3. To make the nose roll the 3"x4" construction paper into a tube and paste. Cut slits a half inch apart around one edge and fold back. Use these to attach to face.

4. Using the various scraps of construction paper, cut the facial features. It is best to cut two at a time so they will match. Then paste onto the nylon stocking. Here are some suggestions:

5. Anything else can be added such as a hat, hair, glasses, a mustache and so forth. These can be made from scraps of construction paper, material, buttons, or yarn.

AUTUMN LEAVES

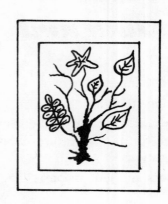

Materials:
1. old peeled crayons
2. fresh leaves with prominent veins
3. brown tempera paint
4. straws (one for each child)
5. (1) 9"x12" white paper

Steps:
1. Put a few drops of thin brown tempera paint on the white paper.

2. Blow lightly at the paint with the straw. Move the paper and change the direction you blow from several times. Add more paint if needed.

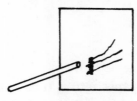 

3. Let paint dry.
4. Put a leaf on the table with the vein side up. Put the white paper with the blown paint on top and *rub* lightly *with the side of the crayon* to pick up the vein pattern of the leaf.

5. Vary colors and shapes of leaves.

CRAYON PAPER BATIK

Materials:

1. crayons
2. (1) 9″x12″ white or manila paper
3. brown tempera paint
4. wide paint brush
5. lots of newspapers
6. running water or a large container of water to dip paper in

Steps:

1. Color a design or picture on the white paper, covering the entire paper. Color heavily, going over an area several times, to build up layers of crayon, not necessarily pressing very hard.

2. Put the paper under running water or in a container of water to make completely wet. Then crumple it into a tight ball so the crayon cracks. Open it up.

3. Lay the wet paper on newsprint and paint over the entire picture with the brown tempera paint.

4. After painting, put the paper back in the water to wash off the paint. Spread out flat on newspaper to dry. When dry, it can be ironed on the back side to make it perfectly flat.

TISSUE LEAF RUBBINGS

Materials:

1. 5″ squares of tissue paper in autumn colors
2. fresh leaves with prominent veins
3. pieces of brown crayon
4. (1) 6″x18″ white construction paper
5. liquid starch in a small container
6. paint brush and paper towel

Steps:

1. Put a leaf on the table with the vein side up. Place a single piece of tissue paper on the top of the leaf and rub over the top of the leaf *with the side of the crayon.* This will pick up the vein pattern.

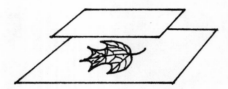 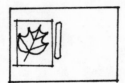

2. Repeat step one on different colors of tissue paper. Then tear out the leaf shape rubbing on each piece of paper.

3. Using the paint brush, cover the 6″x18″ white construction paper with liquid starch. One at a time, lay the tissue leaves on the paper, covering each piece with liquid starch before adding another.

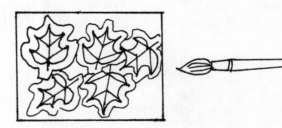

SIMPLE OWL

Materials:

1. (1) 9"x12" brown construction paper
2. (2) 3"x3" yellow construction paper
3. (1) 1½"x1½" yellow or orange construction paper (for beak)
4. (2) 3"x3" white construction paper
5. (2) 2"x2" black construction paper
6. scissors and paste or glue

Steps:

1. Fold the 9"x12" brown construction paper in half so it is 4½"x12". Cut the corners off, as illustrated, to make the owl's body.

2. Fold the two 3"x3" yellow squares in half, together, and cut the feet. Using the 1½"x1½" square, cut a triangle for the beak.

3. Fold the white and black construction paper squares in half and round off the top, open corners to make the eyes. Paste the black circles inside the white circles. The eyes can look in any direction.

4. Paste all the parts onto the body. The feet should be pasted on the back of the body.

Hints:

—These owls can be made in all sizes and shapes; determined by the size rectangle used for the body shape.

—Crayon or paints can be used to add individuality to the owl.

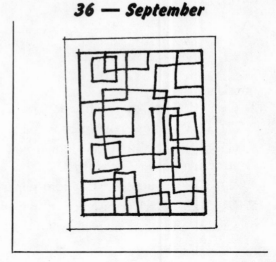

GEOMETRIC DESIGNS

Materials:

1. (1) 6"x9" or 9"x12" white paper
2. a black crayon
3. a set of watercolor paints and brush
4. container of water
5. paper towels

Steps:

1. Select one geometric shape, such as a square, circle or triangle, and using the black crayon, draw that shape on the paper. Repeat it all over the paper in various sizes. Press heavily so the lines are thick and dark.

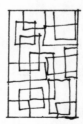 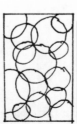 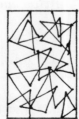

2. Using the watercolors, paint the shapes with watercolors, using many colors.
3. When completed, let it dry thoroughly and mount on construction paper of a complementary color.

LEAF PRINTS

Materials:

1. dark paper, any size
2. thin tempera paint
3. flat container and a sponge for a printing pad
4. fresh leaves with prominent veins

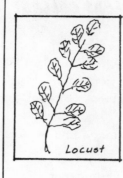
Locust

Avocado

Steps:

1. Place the sponge in a flat container and pour the thin tempera paint over it. This will act as a printing pad.

2. Place the leaf on the printing pad, vein side down, and press gently to pick up paint.

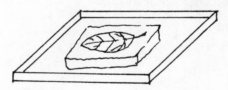

3. Carefully pick up the leaf and lay on a pad of newspapers, paint side up. Place the printing paper on top of the leaf and rub gently.

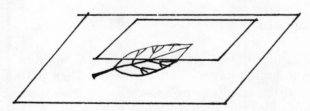

4. Lift the paper off, turn face up and allow to dry.

Hints:

—This could be used as a science project, using the labeled leaf prints to make a notebook.
—Experiment with porous paper such as rice paper, light paint on dark paper or paint on light paper.

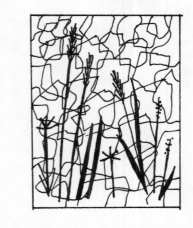

TISSUE AND WEEDS COLLAGE

Materials:
1. dried weeds, long, thin, feathery
2. 4"x4" squares of tissue paper: light blue, shades of green, browns, and yellows
3. white glue and water, ½ and ½
4. paint brush
5. (1) 9"x12" heavy white paper

Steps:

1. Tear the squares of tissue paper into pieces of various sizes and shapes.

2. Paint the 9"x12" heavy white paper with a coat of the glue mixture. Put on some of the pieces of tissue paper, covering each piece with a coat of the glue mixture. (Keep in mind a landscape, putting the blue tissue at the top of the paper for sky and the other colors lower to give the impression of land, etc.)

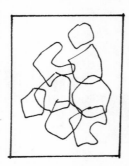

3. Make sure the entire paper has a good coat of the glue mixture and then arrange the dried weeds in a desired pattern over the tissue. Then put on pieces of tissue paper over the top of the dried weeds. Be sure to cover each piece of tissue paper with the glue mixture. Put on several layers of tissue.

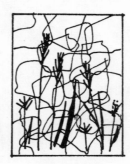

WEAVING PAPER

Materials:

1. (1) 12″x18″ construction paper of any color
2. strips of construction paper of various width, 12″ long
3. scissors and paste or glue

Steps:

1. Fold the 12″x18″ colored construction paper in half, widthwise. Draw a pencil line one inch down from the open edge. Cut curved, straight or zig-zag lines from the folded edge to the pencil line. (These lines can be penciled in first.)

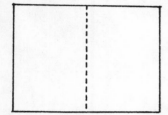 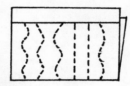 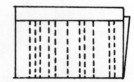

2. Cut zig-zag or curved edges on the strips of various widths. Use straight-edged strips as well.

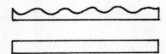 

3. Weave the 12″ long strips across the width of the paper. Experiment by leaving spaces, going under one, over three, and so forth.

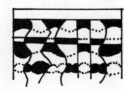 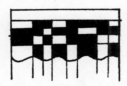

4. When the weaving is completed, paste down all the ends of the strips and trim the edges so they will be straight.

WHITE SAILS

Materials:

1. 5″x5″ squares of tissue paper—light blue, dark blue, green
2. liquid starch in a small container
3. paint brush
4. (1) 9″x12″ white construction paper
5. (1) 6″x9″ white construction paper
6. scissors and glue or paste

Steps:

1. Tear the 5″x5″ squares of tissue paper into small pieces.
2. Cut white sailboat shapes out of the 6″x9″ white construction paper.

3. Cover the 9″x12″ white paper with a coat of liquid starch, using the paint brush. Lay on the pieces of torn tissue paper, light blue pieces at the top and dark blue and green pieces at the bottom, to give the impression of sky and water. Cover with more starch. Let dry.

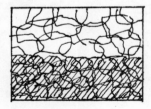

4. When the tissue background is dry, paste or glue the white sailboats to the paper.

October

EXPLORER'S SHIP

Materials:

1. (1) small milk carton
2. (1) ice cream stick
3. (2) 4½"x6" brown construction paper
4. (1) 4½"x6" white construction paper
5. scraps of paper for decoration
6. scissors and glue or paste

Steps:

1. Using the scissors, trim the milk carton so it will be about 2½" high. Glue the ice cream stick to the inside of one end of the carton.

2. Put the two 4½"x6" pieces of brown construction paper together and cut out the ship as illustrated. Glue the ships to the sides of the milk carton and the ends to each other. This will cover the milk carton.

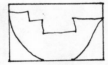 

3. Trim the 4½"x6" piece of white construction paper to make the sail and glue it to the ice cream stick.

4. Decorate the ship and sail with the scraps of paper. Add things such as people in the boat, equipment, symbols on the sail and flags.

PSYCHEDELIC WEAVING

Materials:

1. 2 sheets of different colored construction paper
2. scissors
3. glue or paste

Steps:

1. Take one sheet of construction paper and draw a line the width of the paper with a pencil, one inch from top. Cut curved lines from the bottom to the pencil line. (You can draw curved lines with a pencil first.)

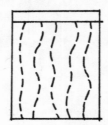

2. Using the second sheet, cut curved strips, *one at a time,* across the width of the paper. Weave each one into the second sheet.

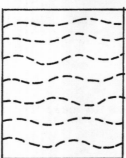 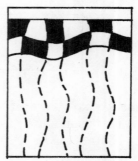

3. Glue down all the ends and trim the edges to make them straight.

Hints:

1. *Be sure to cut only one strip at a time.* This will eliminate any confusion and also loss of strips.
2. This can also be done with 12″x18″ construction paper.

CRAYON ETCHING

Materials:

1. (1) 9″x12″ white construction paper or drawing paper
2. a piece of chalk, yellow or white
3. dark and light crayons; yellow and brown
4. a pencil

Steps:

1. Fold the paper in half and open again.

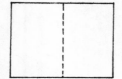 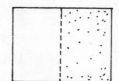

2. On one side rub lightly over the surface with the chalk, covering with a heavy, even coat.

3. Color heavily over the chalk, using a yellow or orange crayon. Color a second layer with a dark crayon, such as black or brown. Be sure to cover the light color completely.

4. Fold the paper closed, and draw a picture on it with a pencil. Press heavily. When finished you will have two pictures. (If the picture did not reverse in some places, it is very easy to fold it closed and draw again, or add to the picture.)

Variations:

—These make marvelous Halloween pictures. They can also be used in the spring for flowers, using pastel colors.

CRAYON ON BLACK DESIGN

Materials:

1. (1) 9"x12" black construction paper
2. many colors of crayons
3. lots of time
4. watercolors (if a wash is desired)

Steps:

1. Begin the design by making dots or points at various intervals all over the black paper with a pencil or crayon.

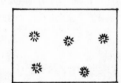

2. Around each point or dot, with any color, make a circle with short, straight lines. Do this around each dot or point on the paper.

3. Continue by putting another ring around each circle with another color. Keep adding more rings of short, straight lines around each circle, changing the color for each ring.

4. When the circles begin to touch each other decide which ones will complete their circles and stop the rings of the other circles where they meet.

5. Stop when the paper is completely filled. As an added activity, a watercolor wash of a bright color can be painted over the entire paper to create an unusual effect.

OWL PUPPET

Materials:

1. brown construction cut to these sizes:
   (1) 9"x12"   (2) 3"x6"   (2) 2½"x2½"
2. (2) 3"x3" yellow construction paper
3. (1) 4"x5" tan construction paper
4. scraps of orange and yellow paper for eyes and a beak
5. scissors and paste or glue

Steps:

1. Put paste on one side of the 9"x12" brown construction paper and roll into a tube. Hold firmly. Put paste on the inside of the tube about two inches down and pinch top together.

2. Cut the 3"x6" pieces of brown construction paper into wing shapes. (Cut both at the same time.) Paste to the tube in the middle of the back. For the chest, fold tan paper and cut shape as shown. Paste on the lower front of tube.

3. Cut the 3"x3" yellow construction paper into feet. Fold the top part down about 1", paste and attach to body.

4. Fold the scraps to cut eyes and a beak.

5. Fold the 2½"x2½" piece of brown paper in half and cut ears.

6. Paste all parts onto tube as shown, after trimming off top corners of the tube to make the head shape.

WHITE ON BLACK FINGERPAINTING

Materials:

1. black butcher paper, or construction paper, any size
2. liquid starch
3. white powdered tempera paint
4. newspaper

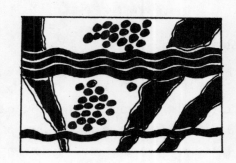

Steps:

1. Place the black paper on newspaper to protect the working surface.

2. Pour about three tablespoons of liquid starch on the center of the black paper. Sprinkle on about one tablespoon of white powdered tempera paint.

3. Smear the starch and paint with the drawing hand, mixing together thoroughly. Cover the entire page, making sure to get the corners.

4. Create any design desired. This is excellent for experimenting and discovering lines and textures which can be made with the fingers. Here are a few suggestions:

fingernails   edge of hand   side of hand   fingertips

Variations:

—Draw pictures for Halloween.

DANCING WITCH

Materials:

1. construction paper: black and skin color
2. scissors and glue or paste
3. thin string
4. Scotch or masking tape
5. black crayon

Steps:

1. Cut out 2 bodies, 2 heads, 4 legs, 1 circle, 4 shoes and 2 hands. (see suggested shapes)

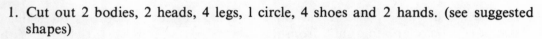

2. Draw a face on the circle with crayons.

3. Glue circle onto head, shoes onto legs and hands onto body.

4. Turn both sets of parts face down on the table and lay next to each other in the order that they will hang.

5. Tape a long piece of string from the top of the hat to the body and short pieces from the body to each leg. (You can also paste the string into position as the top pieces will hold the strings into place)

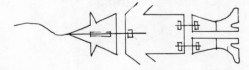

6. Glue the other set of parts over to cover the string and tape.

BOUNCING SKELETON

Materials:

1. (1) 8½"x11" white construction paper
2. (4) 4½"x11" thin, white paper
3. (1) 6"x9" white construction paper
4. (2) 6"x9" black construction paper
5. scissors and paste or glue

Steps:

1. Fold the 8½"x11" construction paper in half, lengthwise. Do this three times. Cut slits on alternating sides from the fold, ½" apart, almost to the edge of the opposite side. Open carefully and flatten, but do not pull open.

2. Fold the 4½"x11" pieces of thin, white paper in half, twice. Since the paper is thin, two pieces can be folded and cut together. Cut slits on alternating sides, as in step 1.

3. Fold the 6"x9" white construction paper in half and cut the skeleton's head. Fold the 6"x9" pieces of black paper in half and cut feet or shoes and hands. Use crayons or scraps of black paper for the facial features.

4. Glue or paste the 4 narrow pieces of thin, white paper to the larger pieces of white construction paper to form the body. These will be the arms and legs. Glue or paste on the head, hands and feet. The hands and feet will weigh down the arms and legs and pull the slits apart to make the skeleton bounce.

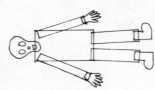

FLYING BAT

Materials:

1. (1) 4″x4″ square of black construction paper
2. (2) 2″x9″ black construction paper
3. scraps of colored paper for eyes
4. scissors and paste
5. string to hang

Steps:

1. Fold the 4″x4″ square in half and cut off the corners to make a circle. Open and cut half way up the fold to the center. Overlap edges and paste.

2. Place the two 2″x9″ pieces of construction paper on top of each other. Cut off the top corners and the lower parts of the wings as illustrated.

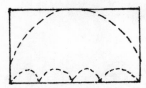

3. Paste the wings to the back part of the head.

4. Cut eyes, nose, etc., from scraps of construction paper and paste onto head.
5. Staple or paste a piece of string to the head so that the bat can be hung.

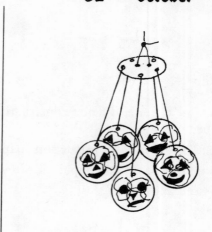

JACK-O-LANTERN MOBILE

Materials:

1. clear plastic lids from cans such as coffee, any size
2. shades of orange tissue paper, scraps or squares, 3"x3"
3. scraps of black construction paper
4. white glue mixture; ½ water, ½ glue
5. paint brush, scissors
6. string or thread and a paper punch

Steps:

1. Tear the pieces of orange tissue paper into small pieces, different shapes. Using the scraps of black construction paper, cut the facial features for the jack-o-lanterns.

2. Lay the plastic lids on newspaper. Paint one side with the glue mixture and put on the pieces of tissue paper, covering each piece with some of the glue mixture. While still wet lay on eyes, nose, and mouth. Make one lid plain orange from which to hang the others. Let dry.

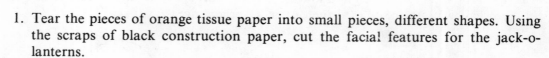

3. Punch holes in the orange lid for each jack-o-lantern to be hung. Punch two holes next to each other in the center and slip through a string to hang the mobile. Punch one hole in the top of each jack-o-lantern, tie a string to each and then tie the other ends of strings to the hanging lid.

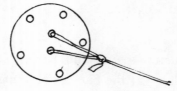 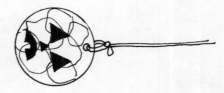

JACK-O-LANTERN

Materials:

1. (1) 9″x12″ orange construction paper
2. (1) 9″x12″ black construction paper
3. scissors
4. paste

Steps:

1. Fold the orange construction paper in half, widthwise. Using a pencil, draw half a jack-o-lantern with center on the fold. Cut out.

 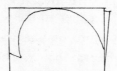

2. Holding the fold, cut rings out of center of jack-o-lantern. Cut around to top, *almost to fold,* and then turn around and cut back to fold. (See illustration) Cut two or three rings.

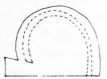  

3. To cut features:

   eyes: fold center section and cut eye shape

   nose and mouth: cut on center fold

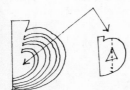

4. Paste the jack-o-lantern onto the black construction paper. (You can also paste on black butcher paper and add background with colored chalk)

GHOST PAINTING

Materials:

1. (1) white construction paper, 18″x12″ or 9″x12″
2. wax paper (same size as white paper)
3. pencil with a dull point
4. water color paints or thin tempera paint (2 colors)
5. paint brush (at least 1″ wide)
6. water

Steps:

1. Place wax paper over the white construction paper. (You can tape or paper clip them together so the wax paper won't slide around)
2. Draw a picture on the wax paper with the dull pencil, *pressing down hard.*
3. Remove the wax paper. The wax will have transferred to the paper.
4. Paint over the entire picture with a very light, thin color (such as orange). Paint lightly with tip of brush, never scrubbing. Do not go over picture more than once.
5. Without waiting for the first coat to dry, go over the picture with a dark color (such as purple). Don't worry about covering the paper smoothly—let it streak.
6. To make the torn paper frame, use a piece of construction paper the same size as the picture. Fold the paper in half and tear the center out about 1½″ from the edge. Open and paste onto picture.

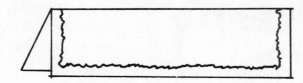

Hints:

1. Use very, very thin paint.
2. Use good, heavy wax paper
3. Only paint over once; don't go back and forth over picture.

RUBBER CEMENT GHOSTS

Materials:

1. (1) 9"x12" white paper
2. rubber cement glue with a small brush
3. water color paints and paint brush
4. small container of water

Steps:

1. Lightly pencil in ghosts of all shapes and sizes all over the paper. (Any other Halloween picture can be used as long as the picture is not too detailed.) Paint rubber cement over the ghosts, leaving spaces for the eyes. Make sure the rubber cement is on quite thick.

2. After making sure the rubber cement is completely dry, paint over the whole paper with watercolors. Various shades of black can be used or any combination of colors desired. The paint will not take very well over the rubber cement.

3. When the paint is thoroughly dry, rub off the rubber cement gently with the tips of the fingers or an eraser. The ghosts will pop out white against the painted background.

CHALK STENCIL GHOSTS

Materials:

1. (1) 9"x12" black paper
2. (1) 3"x4½" heavy paper for stencil
3. chalk dust from chalkboard or scraped from a piece of chalk
4. a piece of cotton or kleenex
5. scissors and pencil with eraser

Steps:

1. Fold the 3"x4½" heavy piece of paper in half. Cut out a shape for the ghost on the fold. Keep the outside piece for the stencil.

2. Lay the stencil on top of the black paper and hold it down firmly with one hand. Dip the piece of cotton or end of the kleenex in the chalk dust and then smear over the edges of the stencil, rubbing from the outside edge to the middle.

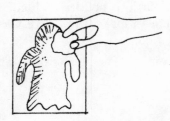

3. Make ghosts all over the paper, upside down and overlapping. The children can also exchange stencils.
4. Make eyes in each ghost by using the tip of an eraser.

JACK-O-LANTERN FINGERPAINTING

Materials:

1. white butcher paper or fingerpainting paper
2. black butcher paper
3. orange tempera paint
4. liquid starch
5. scissors, and glue or paste

Steps:

1. Cut white butcher paper into large pieces the size you wish the jack-o-lanterns
   to be.
2. Fingerpaint one large jack-o-lantern on the white butcher paper, using the
   liquid starch and paint.
3. When the jack-o-lantern is dry, cut it out. Also cut out the eyes, mouth and
   nose.
4. Paste or glue the jack-o-lantern onto a large sheet of black butcher paper. Trim
   around the edge of the jack-o-lantern, leaving a black border around the edge.

Variations:

1. Make the background orange and the jack-o-lantern black.
2. Use for border decorations, windows, etc.

Hints:

1. Pour starch onto the white paper and then sprinkle on the tempera. Children
   can mix with their hands.
2. Fingerpaint with one hand only. It's not as messy and children will have one
   clean hand to pick-up, etc.
3. Before pasting the jack-o-lanterns on the black paper flatten under a stack of
   books over night if they have a tendency to curl.

SPOOKY PICTURE

Materials:

1. tissue paper in shades of orange and yellow
2. small container of liquid starch
3. white construction paper
   (1) 12"x18"   (1) 9"x12"
4. One sheet black construction paper, 12"x18"
5. scissors and paste or glue
6. paint brush

Steps:

1. Cut or tear tissue paper into various shapes.
2. Using the paint brush, paint liquid starch on the 12"x18" paper; lay on tissue pieces one at a time, painting over each with a coat of starch. Let dry.
3. For the frame, fold the black paper in half, 6"x18", and tear out frame. Start and end on the folded edge.

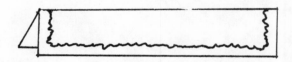

4. Paste the frame onto the 12"x18" white paper, covered with tissue paper.

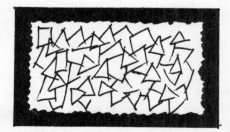

5. Cut out ghosts, jack-o-lanterns, etc., from the white construction paper and paste onto tissue design. Be sure to cut out eyes, mouth, etc., so that the tissue paper will show through.

BOX JACK-O-LANTERN

Materials:

1. a box, any size
2. orange tempera paint
3. wide paint brush
4. scraps of black and green construction paper
5. scissors and paste or glue

Steps:

1. Paint the box orange with the tempera paint. To make sure the paint will cover any printing on the box, add some liquid soap to the tempera paint.
2. When the box is dry, use the black construction paper scraps to make eyes, a nose and a mouth. Paste or glue onto the box. Use the green construction paper to make a stem. Paste or glue to the top of the jack-o-lantern.

Hints:

—To make sure the paint will not rub off the boxes, spray with lacquer, varnish, or hair spray. Do this before adding the facial features.
—Make a large stack of jack-o-lanterns for the classroom, using each child's jack-o-lantern

BLACK CAT

Materials:

1. (1) 9″x12″ piece of black construction paper
2. scraps of red and green paper
3. scissors and paste or glue

Steps:

1. Fold the black construction paper in half, widthwise. Cut body as shown in the illustration. Set aside.

 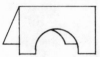

2. Trim a bit from the curved part of the left over paper for tail.

3. Trim two small, thin pieces for whiskers.

4. Cut out nose and mouth from red scraps. Cut eyes from green scraps. Paste on head, attaching whiskers when pasting on nose.

5. Glue, paste or staple the head and tail to the body. (This cat will stand by itself when finished)

Hints:

1. Make a calico cat by using gray bogus paper and coloring designs all over it.

CAT MASK

Materials:

1. (1) 10″x10″ black construction paper
2. (2) 2″x2″ squares of black construction paper
3. (2) 1″x1½″ green construction paper
4. (1) 1½″x1½″ green construction paper
5. narrow strips of black construction paper for whiskers
6. scissors and paste

Steps:

1. Fold the 10″x10″ black construction paper in half and trim the corners of the open edge to make a circle.

2. Place the 2″x2″ black construction squares on top of each other and fold in half. Cut diagonally from one corner to the opposite corner, to make the ears.

3. Use the green construction paper pieces to make eyes and the red for a nose. Curve the corners off.

4. Open the circle and lay flat on the desk. In the very center put paste, lay on whiskers, and then the nose. Paste on eyes and ears. Cut up the fold almost to the nose. Pull one edge over the other and paste so the mask curves around the face.

MARTIAN MASK

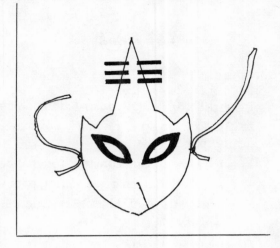

Materials:

1. (1) 12″x18″ construction paper, any color
2. (1) 2″x12″ construction paper, same color as the 12″x18″ piece
3. (3) 1″x4″ construction paper for antennae
4. (2) 2″x4″ construction paper for eyes
5. scissors and paste or glue

Steps:

1. Fold the 12″x18″ piece of construction paper in half and cut out the shape of the mask as illustrated. Cut slits for the antennae.

2. Fold the 2″x4″ pieces of construction paper together lengthwise; trim the corners to make a leaf shape. Then cut a smaller leaf shape inside and keep the leaf shape rings.

3. Open the mask shape and lay flat on the desk. Slide the 1″x4″ construction paper strips through the slits for the antennae. Paste the leaf shape rings at a slant where the eyes will be. Then cut eye holes inside the rings.

4. Cut a 2″ slit on the fold at the bottom of the mask. Slide the cut edges over each other about 2″ and paste so that the nose sticks out.

5. Paste the 2″x12″ strip of construction paper to the back of the mask at eye level and slip over the head to wear

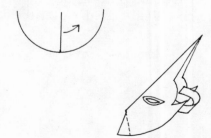

EGG CARTON MASKS

Materials:

1. (1) '2 egg-section' from a cardboard egg carton
2. (2) 12' pieces of string
3. scraps of paper, ribbon, string
4. scissors and glue

Steps:

1. CUTTING THE EGG CARTON: 5 masks can be cut from each egg carton; each mask will have two cups for the eyes and a pointed section for the nose. Cut as illustrated by the heavy line in the illustration below:

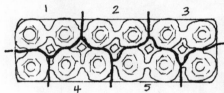

2. Using the points of a scissors, cut an eye hole in each cup. Poke a small hole on each side of the mask and attach the strings so that the mask can be tied on.

3. Decorate the mask by cutting out hats, a mustache, flowers, glasses, beards, hair and anything else desired. Children will be most ingenious at decorating them once they are shown how to attach the various things to the egg carton.

   a. glue any kind of hat to the top of the mask
   b. hang hair down the sides and curl by pulling the strips through the fingers
   c. make eyes like springs that pop out the sockets or eyelashes.

HANDLE MASK

Materials:

1. (1) 4½"x9" construction paper, any color
2. (1) l"x12" strip heavy cardboard or a 12" long reed
3. scraps of paper, yarn, fabric
4. scissors and paste or glue

Steps:

1. Fold the 4½"x9" piece of construction paper in half, widthwise, and draw on half the mask shape desired. Remember to draw eye holes. Cut out.

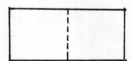 

2. Glue or paste the cardboard strip to one side of the mask. If using a 12" reed, tape to side of mask.

3. Decorate the mask with the scraps of paper, yarn and fabric. It can be made scary, funny, beautiful or any way desired.

 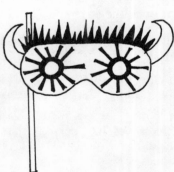

November

PUZZLE PICTURE

Materials:

1. (2) 9″x9″ pieces of white paper
2. crayons and a pencil
3. scissors and paste or glue

Steps:

1. Using the pencil, draw the outline of a simple picture on one piece of white paper. Be sure to draw over the entire paper and make the lines fairly heavy.

2. Cut the picture up into about eight to ten pieces, completely disregarding the design or illustration.

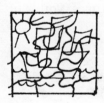

3. Color all the pieces separately with any colors desired. Each piece will have several divisions and each should be colored with different colors.
4. When the coloring is completed, put the puzzle back together and paste onto the other 9″x9″ white paper.

Hints:

—It is best to work with only four to five colors.
—This is an excellent way to make a class mural, having groups of three or four children working on each section.

CRAYON RUBBING

Materials:

1. various size pieces of tagboard or any other heavy paper
2. various sizes of colored newsprint
3. old peeled crayons
4. scissors

Steps:

1. Using the tagboard, cut out figure such as a girl jumping rope or walking or any shape desired.

  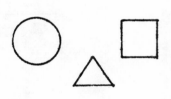

2. Place the cutout under a sheet of newsprint.
3. Rub over the figure with the side of a crayon on the newsprint. Move the figure slightly to overlap and repeat. Do this several times. After you have repeated this process a number of times you will have a group of figures jumping.

Variations:

1. Experiment with a variety of shapes such as trees, flowers, animals, people in motion.
2. You can also reverse the process and lay the figure on top of the paper. Rub the crayon from the center of the cutout over the outside edge onto the newsprint.
3. This is also a good lesson of how to give depth to a picture by overlapping figures.

CRAYON SCREEN PRINTING

Materials:

1. a piece of thin, cotton fabric
2. wax crayons or white glue
3. a piece of cardboard or chipboard
4. powdered tempera paint mixed with liquid starch, very thick
5. newsprint
6. scissors and masking tape
7. cardboard square, 1"x2"
8. matt knife or single-edged razor blade for teacher

Steps:

1. Measure a border of at least one inch around the edge of the cardboard. Using the matt knife or razor blade, cut out the center of the cardboard.

2. Cut a piece of cotton fabric the size of the hole, plus a ½" border. Glue to the bottom of the cardboard. Use masking tape to seal the top edge of cardboard and material.

3. Draw a design or picture on material. Keep it simple. Using crayons or white glue, fill in all areas of the design not to be printed.

4. To print, place frame on paper. Drop a small amount of the thick tempera paint in the middle of the frame. Push the paint back and forth over the design with the 1"x2" cardboard.

5. When all is covered, lift the frame very carefully. The frame can be used to print many times if it is wiped clean after each use.

WEAVING WITH WEEDS

Materials:

1. tall grasses and weeds, at least 6 inches long
2. a shoe box lid
3. string or yarn
4. scissors
5. other materials which could be added: yarn, paper strips, fabric strips

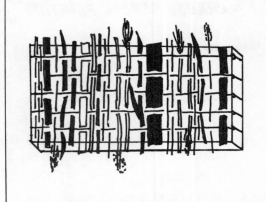

Steps:

1. Cut notches at ½" intervals on the short edges of the shoe box lid.

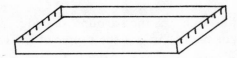

2. Wrap the string or yarn around the box. Begin by tying a knot in the end of the string or yarn and secure it behind the first notch. End the same way.

3. Weave in and out of the strings using the weeds. Don't worry about the ends of the weeds hanging over the edge. Pieces of yarn, ribbon, paper and fabric can be added to give variety if desired.

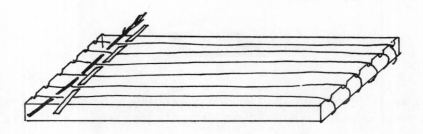

FOLDED OWL

Materials:

1. (1) 9"x9" brown construction paper
2. (2) 3"x3" white construction paper
3. (2) 2"x2" black construction paper
4. (2) 3"x3" orange construction paper
5. scissors and paste or glue

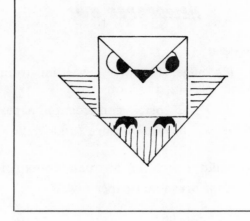

Steps:

1. Fold the 9"x9" brown construction paper in half, diagonally. Open and fold diagonally in the opposite direction. Open and lay flat. Fold each corner point to the center point.

2. Open all corners and lay flat. Put paste or glue on the tip of one corner, fold to the center and press down. Cut off the top small triangle on each side of the folded section. Fringe the remaining triangles.

3. Fold the black and white construction paper squares in half and trim off the open corners to make the eyes. Paste the white circles to the body of the owl, slipping partly under the folded section. Add the black circles, making the owl look in any direction desired.

4. Fold the orange squares in half and cut the feet. Paste the feet onto the fold above the tail. Add a small orange triangle for the beak.

NEWSPAPER OWL

Materials:

1. 1/4 page (11"x14") newsprint from the classified section
2. (1) 9"x12" black construction paper
3. black, brown, orange and yellow chalk
4. liquid starch in a small container
5. paint brush and paper towel

Steps:

1. Fold the newsprint in half. Using a dark crayon draw the outline of an owl on the fold; draw a capital B, add wings, ears and a tail. Cut out.

 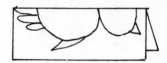

2. Using the paint brush, cover the 9"x12" black construction paper with starch. Lay the newspaper owl on the paper and cover with a coat of starch.

3. Outline the shape of the owl and draw in the feathers and wings with the black or brown chalk. Add any details with the colored chalk such as orange and yellow feathers, black eyes and a yellow beak.

STAR DESIGN

Materials:

1. red and blue crayons
2. (1) 9"x12" piece of white drawing paper
3. 2" of ribbon or string

Steps:

1. Teach the children to draw free form stars.

 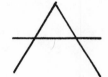 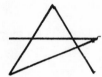 

2. Draw stars of various sizes in red and blue all over the white drawing paper. Color the stars in solid.

3. Draw alternating red and blue lines around each star. Fill in all the small spaces that are created with red and blue.

EGG CARTON UNCLE SAM

Materials:
1. (4) cups from egg carton
2. blue and skin color tempera paint
3. (1) 2"x4" white construction paper
4. (1) 1"x5" blue construction paper
5. (1) 2"x2" blue construction paper
6. (1) 3"x3" black construction paper
7. scraps of white yarn, paper, ribbon
8. scissors and glue

Steps:

1. Trim the edges of the four egg cartons. Glue two together for the body and two together for the head. Glue head to the body. Paint body blue and head skin color with tempera paint.

2. Fold the 3"x3" black construction paper in half and cut a heart for the feet. Glue to the body.

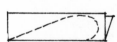

3. Use the 1"x5" blue construction paper strip for the arms, adding hands, cut from scraps. Glue the center of the strip to the back of the body.

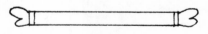

4. Color or paste red strips on the 2"x4" white paper. Paste and roll into a tube. Cut evenly spaced slits up one edge, fold back and paste to the brim. To cut the brim, fold the 2"x2" blue construction paper in half and trim off the open corners.

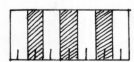

5. Use the scraps of white yarn to make hair and a beard. Glue to the head. Glue on the hat. Add other decorations with the scraps.

TOMAHAWK

Materials:

1. (1) 6"x4½" gray bogus paper or gray construction paper
2. (1) 12"x12" brown construction paper
3. 2' of ribbon or string
4. scraps of construction paper for feathers
5. scissors and glue

Steps:

1. Roll the 12"x12" brown construction paper into a tight stick and glue the edges down.

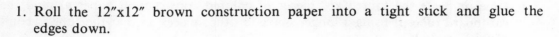

2. Draw the shape of a tomahawk stone on the gray paper. Remember to make two notches so it can be attached to the stick. Cut out.

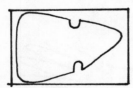

3. Make two 3" slits down the edge from the top on the rolled stone into the slices and fasten by wrapping the ribbon or string around the stick and stone.

  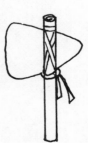

4. Make paper feathers from the scraps of construction paper and glue to the ends of the string or ribbon. Any other decorations desired can be added.

TOTEM POLE

Materials:

1. a cardboard tube
2. (4) 3″x6″ pieces of construction paper of various colors
3. scraps of construction paper, yarn, fabric, old buttons, feathers
4. crayons
5. scissors and paste or glue

Steps:

1. Glue or paste the four 3″x6″ pieces of colored construction paper around the cardboard tube. If using a longer one add other pieces so that the tube is completely covered.

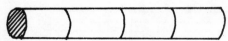

2. Using the scraps of construction paper, cut out wings, noses, ears and hands. Remember to make tabs so they can be pasted or glued to the tube. Make each individual section different.

3. Add details with crayons, shiny paper, buttons, feathers, and anything else desired.

INDIAN HEADRESS

Materials:

1. (1) 2″x24″ or (2) 2″x12″ brown construction paper
2. (1) 2″x36″ or (3) 2″x12″ brown construction paper
3. (10-15) 3″x9″ construction paper, any color for feathers
4. scissors, crayons, paste or glue

Steps:

1. Use the 2″x24″ piece of brown construction paper (or two 2″x12″ pieces pasted together) to make a headband that fits around the head. Glue it together at the proper size and cut away the extra paper.

2. Decorate the 2″x36″ piece of brown construction paper (or three 2″x12″ pieces pasted together) with Indian designs, using the crayons

3. Fold the 3″x9″ pieces of colored construction paper in half. Trim the open edges to make feathery shapes. Cut even slits all along the edges to make them feathery.

4. Glue the feathers evenly all along the 2″x36″ strip of construction paper on the back side.

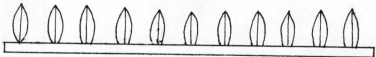

5. Glue the feather strip half way around the headband so the feathers trail down the back.

INDIAN JACKET

Materials:

1. 1 large brown grocery bag
2. scissors
3. crayons, watercolor or tempera paints

Steps:

1. To make the jacket first cut a slit up the middle of the paper bag to the flat part. Cut a neck hole and two holes for the arms, one in each side section.

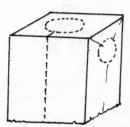

2. Cut slits evenly all the way around the bottom edge to make a fringe.

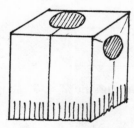

3. To decorate Indian designs can be colored or painted on the jacket. When painting the designs the jacket can be hung on a painting easel to make it easier to paint and dry.

STUFFED INDIAN DOLL

Materials:

1. (2) 12"x18" brown butcher paper or one large grocery paper bag
2. tempera paint or crayons
3. newspapers
4. scissors and glue
5. paper scraps, yarn, fabric

Steps:

1. Fold the two 12"x18" pieces of brown butcher paper in half, together. If using a paper bag, trim the bottom off and then fold in half. Draw on half a person and cut out.

2. Open up and decorate one piece for the front of the doll and the other piece as the back. Use crayons or tempera paint. Use yarn for hair and fabric for clothes. Glue to the paper figure.

3. To stuff, wad up pieces of newspaper into small balls. Roll tubes for the legs and arms. Place the back of the doll, decorated side down, flat on the table. Put glue all around the edge of the doll. Lay on the pieces of wadded newspaper and press on the front part of the doll.

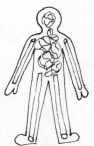

INDIAN

Materials:
1. (1) 9″x12″ brown construction paper
2. (1) 6″x12″ black construction paper
3. (3) 2″x6″ various color for feathers
4. (1) 2″x9″ strip construction paper for headpiece
5. scraps of construction paper for eyes, nose, mouth
6. scissors and paste

Steps:

1. Fold 9″x12″ brown paper in half, widthwise. Cut from the fold to within one inch of open edge, cut evenly spaced slits. Unfold and paste 9″ edges together so the cut strips run up and down.

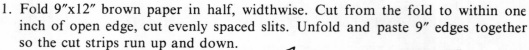

2. For the hair, draw a line 1″ across the top. Cut strips up to the line. Put paste on the 1″ wide section and paste around the lantern shape as shown. If you wish, use scissors or pencil to curl the hair.

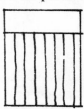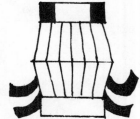

3. For the feather, fold 2″x6″ pieces of construction paper in half and cut a feather shape. Cut slits on the edges.

4. Decorate the headband with crayons or scraps of paper. Paste on feathers to Indian and then paste on the headband.

5. Glue or paste on eyes, nose and mouth.

ROLLED FRUIT

Materials:

1. strips of construction paper, 1″x12″ in various fruit colors
2. glue or paste
3. green paper scraps (for stems and leaves)
4. scissors

Steps:

1. Using one strip, paste ends together to make shape of fruit. (For grapes no shape is needed)

2. Roll the strips and paste down ends. Do enough rolls to fill the shape of the fruit. Put them in shape to test. They can all be different sizes.

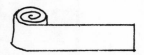 

3. Take out rolls, put paste around edge and replace in fruit shape, sticking all rolls together.
4. Cut out leaves and stems. Paste to the top of the fruit.

Hints:

—Have each child in class make one fruit and then make a class cornucopia for a bulletin board.

MAGAZINE TURKEY

Materials:

1. (1) 12″x12″ construction paper, any color for background
2. scissors
3. paste or glue
4. old magazines

Steps:

1. Have the children cut out separate letters for the body of the turkey, spelling 'roast turkey'.
2. Clip out names of Thanksgiving dinner food items to make the tail and turkey legs.
3. Paste the separate letters to make the main part of the body. Use the words to make the tail. Lay on the paper and arrange before pasting.
4. Finish by drawing the head and feet with a black crayon or cut out of colored construction paper.

3-DIMENSIONAL TURKEY

Materials:
1. (1) 9"x12" light brown construction paper
2. (1) 6"x12" dark brown construction paper
3. 1"x6" strips of yellow, orange and light brown construction paper
4. scissors and paste or glue
5. black crayon

Steps:

1. Draw a turkey body on the dark brown construction paper, freehand, and cut it out.

2. Paste the body onto the light brown construction paper. Draw around the turkey with black crayon and add legs, eyes, and beak.

3. Bend and paste 1"x6" strips of construction paper to make the tail feathers.

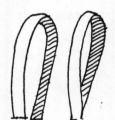

4. Cut out a wing from scraps and paste on turkey to cover strip ends. Cut out a red gobbler and paste to turkey.

TURKEY CUP

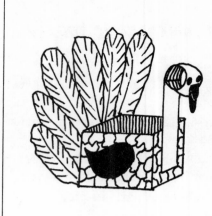

Materials:
1. milk carton
2. scraps of brown construction paper
3. (1) 1″ x 8″ strip of brown construction paper
4. 2″ x 4″ pieces of construction paper for feathers (red, yellow, orange)
5. small pieces of red construction paper
6. scissors and paste

Steps:

1. Cut milk carton in half.

2. Tear small pieces of brown construction paper and paste or glue onto milk carton. (Tearing makes them look more like feathers.)

3. Roll top of 1″ x 8″ brown strip for head and paste.

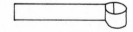

4. Use a black crayon for eyes and scraps of red construction paper to make a gobbler.

5. Paste head onto milk carton.

6. Cut feathers, folding 2″ x 4″ pieces in half, and glue onto milk carton.

TURKEY CARD

Materials:

1. (1) 6″ x 12″ brown construction paper
2. (1) 3″ x 6″ brown construction paper
3. (1) 4½″ x 4½″ brown construction paper
4. 1″ x 6″ strips of construction paper: yellow, orange, tan, red, brown
5. scissors and paste or glue

Steps:

1. Fold the 6″ x 12″ brown construction paper in half. Round off the corners, making sure that it is still attached at the fold.

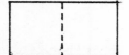   

2. For the head use the 3″ x 6″ brown construction paper. Cut a very fat "L" shape. Round off the corners as shown and cut a slit in the arm of the "L" shape.

3. Round off the corners of the 4½″ x 4½″ brown construction paper and also the 1″ x 5″ strips of all colors. These strips will be the feathers. Slits can be cut to give feathery edges.

  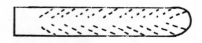

4. Glue or paste all the feathers to the front of the folded body. Stagger and overlap the feathers. Then paste the 4½″ x 4½″ piece over the top to cover the ends of the feathers.

5. Attach the head to the body by folding the tabs in opposite directions on the arm of the "L" and paste. Add the feet, beak and gobbler, made from scraps of construction paper.

STANDING TURKEY

Materials:

1. (1) 6" x 9" light orange or tan construction paper
2. (1) 3" x 9" brown construction paper
3. (1) 1½" x 6" tan construction paper
4. scraps of red, yellow and black construction paper for eyes, beak, gobbler and feet
5. scissors and paste
6. orange, yellow and brown tempera paint poured on sponges in flat containers

Steps:

1. Put sponges in flat containers and pour the tempera paint over the sponges to make paint pads.
2. Place the first four fingers on the paint pads, one color at a time, and print tail feathers on the 6" x 9" light orange construction paper. Remind the children to make the feathers fan out in a half circle. When dry, cut out.

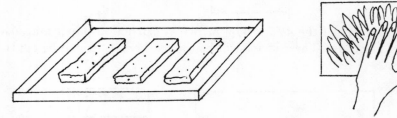

3. Roll the 3" x 9" brown construction paper into a tube and paste. Do the same to the 1½" x 5" light brown construction paper. Paste together to make the head and body. Paste to the tail.

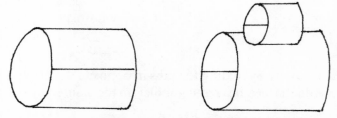

4. Using the scraps of red, black and yellow construction paper, make eyes, beak, gobbler and feet for the turkey. Paste onto the body.

CORNUCOPIA

Materials:

1. tissue paper (brown, purple, blue, yellow, red, orange and green)
2. (1) 9″ x 12″ piece of newsprint
3. (1) 9″ x 12″ white construction paper
4. liquid starch
5. paint brush
6. black crayon

Steps:

1. Cut a cornucopia out of brown tissue paper. Cut various fruit shapes from the other colors of tissue paper.

2. Have children arrange their design first on newsprint.

3. Paint the white construction paper with liquid starch. Move the arrangement from the newsprint to the white paper, one piece at a time. Go over the top of each piece lightly with the liquid starch. Be careful not to go over the edges so the colors won't run.

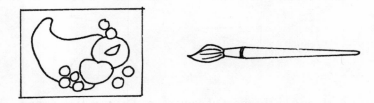

4. Outline the design with crayon after it is dry. The colors of the tissue will have run a bit and this makes it more interesting. Outline the original fruit design.

CORK SHIP MOBILE

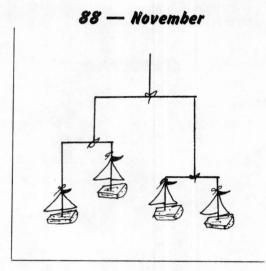

Materials:

1. half a cork, any size for each ship
2. large toothpick, 4″ piece of reed or a pipe cleaner for each ship
3. (2) 2″ x 3″ white construction paper for each ship
4. scraps of construction paper
5. pieces of string or thread
6. 3 pieces of stick or wire
7. scissors and glue

Steps:

1. Poke a hole in the middle of the flat surface of the cork and push in the end of the toothpick, reed or pipe cleaner, covered with a little glue. Hold it until it is secure.

2. Cut two sails from the white construction paper by cutting diagonally across the paper. Cut a flag from the scraps of construction paper. Glue to the mast.

3. Tie a string or thread to the mast of each ship. Then tie the string to the two wires or sticks. Tie a string to middle of the stick or wire to hang the three wire mobile.

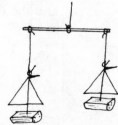

WALNUT PEOPLE

Materials:

1. (1) 9″ x 12″ construction paper, any color for the background
2. one half of a whole walnut shell
3. scraps of fabric, paper, yarn
4. crayons
5. scissors and glue or paste

Steps:

1. Glue the walnut shell to the 9″ x 12″ piece of construction paper. Put it about two inches down from the top, in the middle.

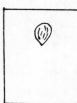

2. Using a crayon or marking pen, draw a face on the walnut shell. Scraps of fabric, paper, yarn and crayons are used to make the body, clothes and other decorations desired.

STANDING GIRL PILGRIM

Materials:

1. skin color construction paper:
   (1) 9″ x 12″   (1) 4″ x 4″
2. white construction paper:
   (1) 9″ x 9″   (2) 2″ x 4″
3. black or gray construction paper
   (2) 2″ x 12″   (1) 7½″ x 10″
4. (1) 9″ x 12″ yellow construction paper
5. scissors and paste or glue, crayons

Steps:

1. Put paste along the 9″ edge of the 9″ x 12″ skin color paper and roll into a tube. Fold the 9″ x 9″ white paper in half and trim off the corners.

2. Set the paper tube on the fold of the white paper and draw half a circle in the center. This will make a fairly accurate hole to slide over the tube for the collar.

3. Paste the 2″ x 12″ strips of paper together. Cut hands from the 4″ x 4″ skin color paper and paste to the arms. Fold the 2″ x 4″ white papers in half and paste on arms for cuffs. Paste the arms to the back of the tube. Slide on collar.

4. Make the hair by cutting even strips up from the edge of the 9″ x 12″ yellow paper and paste to tube. Curl the ends and cut bangs. Make a face with crayons or paper scraps.

5. To make the hat, fold back about a 1½″ strip on the 10″ edge for brim. Roll back the unfolded corners, overlap and paste as shown.

 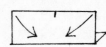

STANDING BOY PILGRIM

Materials:

1. skin color construction paper:
   (1) 9″ x 12″   (1) 4″ x 4″
2. white construction paper
   (1) 9″ x 9″   (1) 2 x 4″
3. black or gray construction paper:
   (1) 7″ x 7″ (2) 2″ x 12″ (1) 7″ x 12″
4. (1) 3″ x 12″ yellow construction paper
5. scissors and paste or glue

Steps:

1. Put paste along the 9″ edge of the 9″ x 12″ skin color paper and roll into a tube. Fold the 9″ x 9″ white paper in half and cut off the corners.

   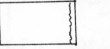

2. Set the paper tube on the fold of the white paper and draw a half circle in the center. This will make a fairly accurate hole to slide over the tube for the collar.

3. Paste the 2″ x 12″ strips of paper together. Cut hands from the 4″ x 4″ skin color paper and paste to ends. Fold the 2″ x 4″ white papers in half and paste on arms for cuffs. Paste the arms to the back of the tube. Paste hands together. Slide on collar.

4. Make the hair by cutting even slits along the edge of the 3″ x 12″ yellow paper and paste to the top of the head. Make a face with crayons or paper scraps.

5. To make the hat, fold the 7″ x 7″ paper in half and cut corners for the brim. Paste and roll the 7″ x 7″ paper into a tube. Cut slits evenly spaced along the back and paste to the hat brim.

December

RUDOLPH PUPPET

Materials:

1. (1) #5 paper bag
2. (2) 6″ x 6″ black construction paper
3. (1) 2″ x 3½″ white construction paper
4. (1) 2″ x 9″ white construction paper
5. (1) 2″ x 2″ red construction paper
6. scraps of white construction paper
7. scissors and paste or glue

Steps:

1. Place the pieces of 6″ x 6″ black construction paper on top of each other. Draw around hand on the top piece and cut out the hand shape. These will be the antlers.

2. Trim the 2″ x 2″ red construction paper to make the nose. Using the white construction paper scraps, cut out all sizes of small circles. Also cut eyes from the paper scraps.

3. Paste or glue the 2″ x 3½″ white construction paper to the bottom of the paper bag. Glue or paste the 2″ x 9″ white construction paper down the middle of the paper bag, remembering to slip it under the flap made by the bottom of the paper bag. Add white dots to sides of the body.

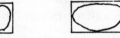

4. Glue or paste the antlers to the back corners of the paper bag as illustrated. Add the eyes and nose.

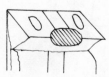

WREATH

Materials:

1. (1) 9" x 12" green construction paper
2. 1½" x 1½" squares of various shades of green tissue paper
3. (1) 4½" x 6" piece of red construction paper
4. scissors and paste or glue

Steps:

1. Fold the green construction paper in half, lengthwise. Draw half a circle ring on the fold, about 3" wide. Cut out and unfold.

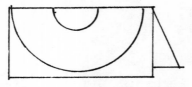

2. Put a drop of white glue or paste on the circle, cover with a tissue paper square and pinch up sides. Do this again and again until the ring is covered. Mix the shades of green tissue as you go along.

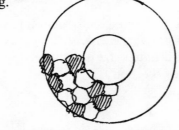

3. Fold the red construction paper in half, widthwise, and cut out a red bow and some berries. Glue or paste onto wreath.

Hint:

This technique can also be used to make ornaments or a Christmas tree.

HAND WREATH

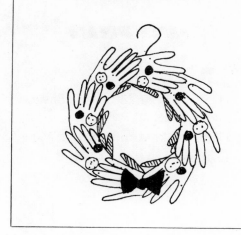

Materials:

1. a wire coat hanger
2. (1) 6″ x 6″ heavy paper for pattern
3. (12) 6″ x 6″ shades of green construction paper
4. scissors and glue or paste
5. scraps of shiny paper, yarn

Steps:

1. Holding the top of the hanger with one hand, pull the bottom of the hanger with the other hand to make the circle shape.

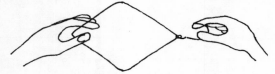 

2. Place one hand on the 6″ x 6″ heavy paper and trace around it to make a hand pattern. Cut out.

3. Using the pattern cut about twelve paper hands from the green construction paper.
4. Put paste on one side of each paper hand and paste to hanger, alternating sides and colors so the hanger will be covered between the paper hands.

5. Decorate the wreath with shiny paper and/or yarn baubles, ribbon and anything else desired.

PAPER WREATH

Materials:

1. (1) 9″ x 12″ or 12″ x 18″ construction paper.
2. (1) 6″ x 9″ red construction paper
3. scissors and paste or glue

Steps:

1. Fold the green construction paper in half, lengthwise. Fold in half again. Open to first fold and cut as you would a lantern. Make sure you are cutting from the fold to the center fold line.

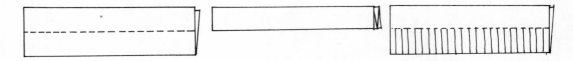

2. Open. Fold the uncut edges over each other and paste. Curve around and slide ends into each other and paste.

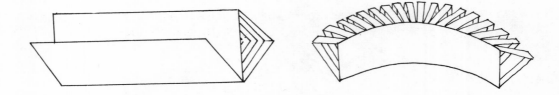

3. To cut the bow, fold the 6″ x 9″ red construction paper in half, widthwise. Using a pencil, draw on half a bow and cut out. Also cut berries from the scraps. Glue onto wreath.

PAPER FRUIT WREATH

Materials:

1. (1) 12″ square of green construction paper
2. scraps of all colors of construction paper for fruit
3. crayons or colored chalk
4. scissors and paste or glue

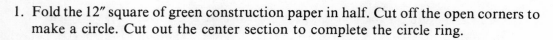

Steps:

1. Fold the 12″ square of green construction paper in half. Cut off the open corners to make a circle. Cut out the center section to complete the circle ring.

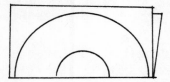 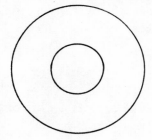

2. Use the scraps of construction paper to make the fruit, which can be in all sizes and shapes. Use the crayons or chalk to outline and accent the fruit. Also cut out leaves and holly.

3. Paste or glue the fruit and leaves to the green paper circle ring. A piece of yarn can be tied or glued to the wreath so that it can be hung.

Variations:

—The fruit can be made from old Christmas cards for a different effect.

—Instead of fruit, symbols of Christmas, such as a bell, candle, candy cane, Santa, and a star can be made and put on the wreath.

SNOW RESIST

Materials:

1. a piece of colored construction paper, any size you wish
2. one crayon the same color as the paper
3. very thin, white tempera paint
4. wide paint brush

Steps:

1. Draw a picture on the colored paper with the crayon, pressing very heavily.
2. Paint over the picture lightly with the white paint. (The paint must be thin enough so that it doesn't cover the crayon, but thick enough so it covers the paper, giving a snow effect.)

Hints:

1. This could be used as a Christmas card.

STAINED GLASS TREE

Materials:

1. (1) 9″ x 12″ black construction paper
2. pieces of tissue paper, all colors
3. a pencil and a ruler
4. scissors and glue or paste

101 — December

Steps:

1. Fold the black construction paper in half, lengthwise. Draw a border, ½″ wide, around the open edges.

2. Draw half a Christmas tree along the fold and a triangle inside each branch section. Join each branch section to the border with a double line.

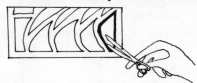

3. Leaving the paper folded, cut out all the spaces around the double-lined design.

4. Open the design and fill in the open spaces with tissue paper. Lay a piece of tissue under the space to be filled and draw around it. Cut out, leaving a ½″ border for pasting. Keep the design symetrical by putting the same color tissue in the corresponding spaces on both sides.

—Any design such as a candle, bell, or angel can be used. Just make sure the design attaches to the ½″ border in some way.

CHRISTMAS PICTURES

Materials:

1. (1) 12″ x 18″ white construction paper (or any size desired if you wish to make a card, etc.)
2. pieces of heavy paper such as gray bogus to make cutouts
3. old, used crayons
4. watercolor paints and brush
5. scissors and pencil
6. container of water and paper towels

Steps:

1. Draw a symbol of Christmas on the heavy paper and cut out. Keep it large and fairly simple. See samples:

  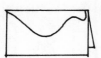 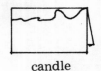

holly   bell   tree   ornament   candle

2. Place the cutout shape under the white paper. Feel with the fingers to locate the shape. *Rub the side of the crayon* over it heavily. Move the cutout and color over it again. Repeat until desired design is created. You can use more than one shape.

3. When the crayon rubbing is completed, give the entire picture a watercolor wash. Use a wide brush and don't paint over the picture any more than is necessary.

STAIN GLASS WINDOW

Materials:

1. (1) 12″ x 18″ black construction paper
2. (1) 12″ x 18″ multi-striped tissue paper
3. a pencil and a ruler
4. scissors and paste or white glue

Steps:

1. Fold the 12″ x 18″ black construction paper in half, widthwise. Fold into thirds. Open so paper is just folded in half and other fold lines are visible. Fold back the end thirds.

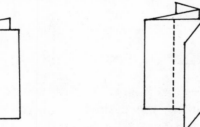

2. Draw a cathedral shaped window on the paper. It can be one single window or three windows. Draw on a ½″ border and designs within the window. Cut out window and designs.

3. Open and lay flat. Put glue or paste on all parts of the black construction paper and then place the 12″ x 18″ piece of multi-colored tissue paper on. When paste or glue is dry trim the edges, cutting away excess tissue.

MACARONI ORNAMENTS

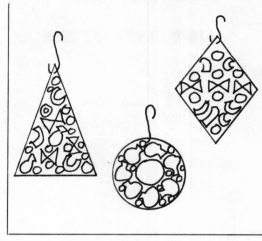

Materials:

1. (1) 3″ x 4″ piece of tagboard or light-weight cardboard for each ornament
2. (1) paper clip for each ornament
3. all shapes and sizes of macaroni
4. scissors and glue
5. gold spray paint and newspapers

Steps:

1. Fold the 3″ x 4″ piece of tagboard or lightweight cardboard in half and cut any shape desired for the ornament.

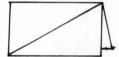  

2. Cover the cutout shape with glue. Arrange macaroni shapes on the ornament. These can be put on in any way desired. When one side is completed let dry. Then turn over and put macaroni on the other side.

3. Put a paper clip through the cardboard to hang.
4. Spray with gold spray paint. It is advisable to lay many ornaments on newspaper and spray all at the same time. Let one side dry, turn over and spray the other side.

FLOUR AND SALT CLAY

Materials:

1. for clay:
   4 cups of flour
   1 cup of salt
   1½ cups of water
2. large bowl to mix clay in
3. a paper clip for each ornament
4. pieces of wax paper and aluminum foil
5. cookie sheet for baking ornaments

Steps:

1. TO MAKE CLAY:
   Mix flour and salt. Add water. Knead exactly as you would bread or clay. The more it is kneaded the better the texture will be. Store in closed plastic bags or containers.

2. USING WITH CHILDREN:
   —Give each child a piece of wax paper to work on and one piece of aluminum foil for the finished ornaments.
   —This clay may be worked with as long as desired since it will not crack nor loose its moisture. Small, tiny details may be added. When the ornament is completed, stick in a small paper clip to be used as a hanger. Place on the tinfoil.

3. TO BAKE:
   —Spray finished ornaments with a fine mist of water. This will make them bake to a golden brown and also assure that all small pieces will stick.
   —Bake at 350° until golden brown or until the pieces move freely on the cookie sheet. Time will depend on the thickness of the ornaments.

4. TO FINISH:
   —Leave natural golden brown and spray with clear shellac, varnish or clear plastic spray paint.
   —Paint designs and patterns with tempera paint and then spray with clear lacquer, varnish or shellac spray paint.

STARCH POINSETTIA

Materials:

1. (6) 2″ x 6″ pieces of red tissue paper, construction paper or fabric
2. (2) 3″ x 5″ green construction paper
3. yellow yarn or paper for centers
4. liquid starch
5. a small, thin tin can
6. scissors

Steps:

1. Fold the 2″ x 6″ pieces of red paper or fabric in half, lengthwise and then widthwise so that they are in quarters. Cut off corners as illustrated.

2. Dip the petals in liquid starch and pull through the fingers to remove excess starch. Drape over the top of the thin, small tin can as illustrated. Let dry thoroughly.

3. Fold the 3″ x 5″ pieces of green construction paper lengthwise and cut leaves.

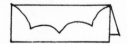

4. Carefully remove dried flower from tin can. Use yellow yarn or paper to make the center for the flower. Glue leaves to the underside of the flower.

CHAINS

Materials:

1. Construction paper in various colors. Cut paper to these measurements: 3″ x 6″ and 3″ x 4″

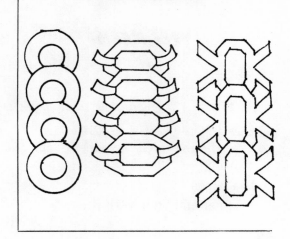

Steps:

1. For all designs, and all sizes, the paper should be folded like this:

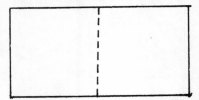

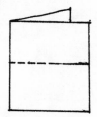

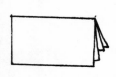

2. Draw designs like this on the folded 3″ x 4″ paper.

3. Draw designs like this on the folded 3″ x 6″ paper.

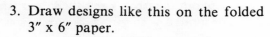

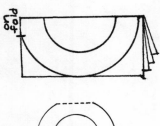

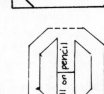

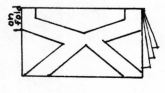

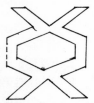

4. After cutting, unfold and hook together, slipping one into the other so the fold hooks the top of the next link.

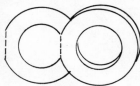

TREE MOBILE

Materials:

1. (1) 9″ x 12″ green construction paper
2. scissors and paste or glue
3. needle and thread or paper punch and string
4. a pencil
5. glitter and sequins (if desired)

Steps:

1. Fold the green construction paper in half, lengthwise. Draw half a tree on the fold and two trees inside this tree.

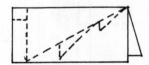 

2. Cut out the trees. Keep the larger tree ring and the solid, center tree. These can be decorated with glitter, sequins or anything else.

3. Using the needle and thread or the paper punch and string, hang the solid tree inside the tree ring and add a string at the top of the tree ring to hang the mobile.

RUDOLPH MASK

Materials:

1. (1) large paper bag
2. (1) 3″ x 3″ red construction paper
3. (2) 1″ x 4″ brown construction paper
4. brown crayon
5. scissors and paste or glue

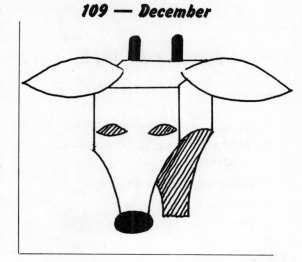

Steps:

1. Open the paper bag and cut out the sides and eye holes as illustrated. Cut the ears from the left over pieces of paper bag.

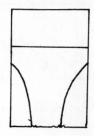

2. Glue or paste the ears to the top of the paper bag.

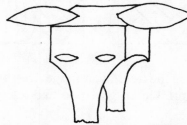

3. Trim off the corners of the 3″ x 3″ red construction paper for the nose. Trim off the corners on one end of the 1″ x 4″ pieces of brown construction paper for the antlers. Glue or paste to the paper bag.

CIRCLE-RING TREE

Materials:

1. (1) 12″ x 18″ white construction paper
2. (6) 3″ x 3″ squares of different colored construction paper
3. scissors and paste or glue
4. pencil
5. glitter

Steps:

1. Fold the 12″ x 18″ white construction paper in half, lengthwise. Draw on half a tree and cut out.

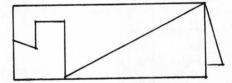 

2. Fold the 3″ x 3″ squares in half and cut out decorations for trees. Cut various shapes. Cut out the center of these shapes. You can get 2 or 3 decorations from every square.

3. Glue or paste decorations on the tree. Overlap the rings and designs. Put on a line of white glue or paste and sprinkle on glitter to make a garland.

4. The tree can be mounted on colored paper

BOUNCING TREE

Materials:

1. (2) 6″ x 6″ squares of green construction paper
2. scraps of colored paper, shiny paper, wrapping paper
3. (1) 2′ piece of green string or yarn
4. scissors and paste

Steps:

1. Cut two big circles the same size from the green construction paper.
2. Cut a circular spring from one of the circles.
3. Paste the first ring of the spring onto the remaining circle.

4. Punch a hole in the center of the circle and thread the yarn through. Tie a knot under the bottom to hold it in place. Tie another knot on the string about 7″ up from the bottom and hook the top of the spring around it.

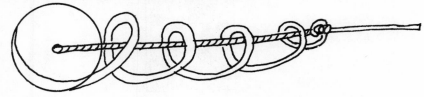

5. Cut out two stars the same size and paste around the string over the top of the tree. Cut out decorations and paste onto the spring.

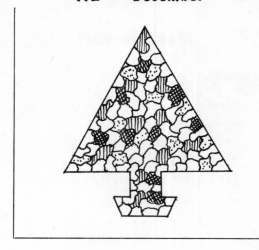

COLLAGE CHRISTMAS TREE

Materials:

1. (1) 9″ x 12″ newsprint
2. (1) 9″ x 12″ construction paper, any color
3. old magazines
4. scissors and pencil
5. paste or glue

Steps:

1. Fold the 9″ x 12″ piece of newsprint in half, lengthwise. Draw on half a tree and cut out. This will be the tree pattern.

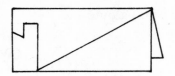

2. Tear bright colored pieces of paper from the old magazines and tear into small shapes. Paste these onto the 9″ x 12″ piece of construction paper. Cover the whole paper, overlapping the pieces. (These can also be applied with liquid starch and a paint brush.) Let dry.

3. Lay the tree pattern on top of the collage and draw around it with a pencil. Cut out the tree. It can then be mounted on a dark or bright colored piece of paper.

LINE TREE

Materials:

1. two colors of construction paper 9″ x 12″
2. paste and scissors
3. pencil

Steps:

1. Fold one piece of construction paper in half, lengthwise. Draw half a tree on the fold and then draw trees inside it 4 or 5 times, following the first tree design.

2. Cut out each tree, starting with the largest tree. You will get a tree ring each time. Open them all up.
3. Take out every other tree ring and put them away.
4. Arrange the remaining trees on the paper, one inside the other, and paste down.
5. You can make two designs, by using the extra tree rings. Arrange them so they are scattered over the paper and overlap each other.

WATERCOLOR SPARKLE TREE

Materials:

1. (1) 6″ x 9″ or 9″ x 12″ white paper
2. watercolor paints and paint brush
3. container of water
4. small sponge, 2″ x 2″
5. piece of construction paper, for tree, 4½″ x 6″ or 6″ x 9″
6. scissors and paste or glue

Steps:

1. Use the sponge to make the white paper wet on both sides.
2. Paint the entire piece of paper green. Place tiny, heavy dots or stars of red, blue and yellow paint all over the paper. Let dry.

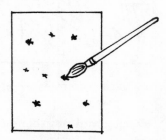

3. Fold the piece of construction paper in half lengthwise. Cut out a tree shape and then cut a tree inside so you will get a tree ring.

4. Glue or paste the tree ring on top of the watercolor design.

SANTA FACES

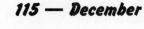

Materials:

1. (1) 12″ x 12″ flesh color construction paper
2. (1) 9″ x 12″ red construction paper
3. white construction paper:
   (1) 9″ x 12″   (1) 2″ x 12″   (1) 3″ x 3″
4. (2) 1½″ x 1½″ blue construction paper
5. (2) 1″ x 1″ black construction paper
6. scissors and paste or glue

Steps:

1. Fold the 12″ x 12″ flesh color construction paper in half and trim off the open corners to make the face.

2. Fold the 9″ x 12″ red construction paper in half, lengthwise, and cut across diagonally, to make the hat. Trim the corners of the 3″ x 3″ white to make a circle. Paste the circle and the 2″ x 12″ whitestrip to the hat.

3. Fold the 9″ x 12″ white construction paper in half, widthwise, and draw on a beard and mustache, as illustrated. Cut out. Fringe the edge of the beard and curl with a pencil.

4. Cut circles from the blue and black construction paper to make eyes. Cut a nose from the red paper scraps. A mouth and cheeks can also be added.

5. Glue or paste all the parts onto the face. First put on the hat, then the beard, mustache and facial features.

STANDING SANTA

Materials:

1. red construction paper cut to the following sizes:
   (1) 4″ x 12″   (1) 2½″ x 9″   (1) 2″ x 4″
2. (1) 2″ x 2½″ skin color paper
3. (1) 4½″ x 6″ black construction paper
4. scraps for eyes, belt, buckle
5. cotton for beard and trim
6. scissors and paste or glue

Steps:

1. Roll the 4″ x 12″ and 2″ x 9″ red construction paper into tubes and paste. Paste the two tubes together.

2. Fold the flesh colored construction paper in half, widthwise, and trim one open corner to make a half circle. Paste to the smaller, top tube for the face.

3. Fold the 2½″ x 4″ red construction paper in half, lengthwise, and cut diagonally across the paper to make the hat. Paste to the top of the face.

4. Fold the 4½″ x 6″ black construction paper in half, widthwise, and draw on feet and hands. Cut out. Paste feet to body. Cut two arms from the red construction paper scraps and paste on arms. Attach arms to inside of bottom tube.

5. Use cotton to make the beard, mustache and trim for the hat and cuffs. Add facial features with scraps or crayons.

SANTA PUPPET

Materials:

1. red construction paper cut to the following sizes:
   1 each: 9" x 12" - body
          6" x 9" -   hat
          3" x 12" - arms
2. (1) 3" x 4" flesh colored construction paper
3. (2) 2" x 2" black construction paper
4. cotton for beard and fur trim.
5. scissors and paste or glue

Steps:

1. Paste one side of the 9" x 12" red construction paper and roll into a tube. On the inside put paste about two inches down and pinch the top together.

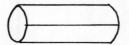 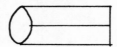

2. Fold the 6" x 9" red construction paper in half, lengthwise, and cut across diagonally to make the hat. Paste or glue to the top of the tube. Put paste in the center of the 3" x 12" red construction paper and attach to the back of the tube.

3. Fold the 3" x 4" flesh colored construction paper in half, widthwise and trim one open corner to make a half a circle, for the face. Paste or glue onto tube below hat.

 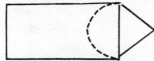

4. Cut arms and feet from the black construction paper. Paste to body. Use cotton for beard, hat trim and cuffs.

FAN SANTA

Materials:

1. (1) 12″ x 18″ red construction paper
2. (1) 9″ x 12″ red construction paper
3. (1) 9″ x 12″ white construction paper
4. scraps of blue and black construction paper
5. scissors and paste

Steps:

1. Fold the 12″ x 18″ red construction paper into a fan. Staple the top to hold securely.

2. Fold the 9″ x 12″ white construction paper in half, widthwise and cut, making scallops all around.

3. Fold the 9″ x 12″ red construction paper in half, lengthwise and cut the hat. This can be any shape.

4. Glue the hat onto the white collar. Add facial features using scraps of black, red and blue construction paper.

5. With the left-over white construction paper cut out round circles for the top of the hat and two hands. Paste onto Santa.

POP OUT CARD

Materials:

1. (1) 6″ x 9″ construction paper
2. (1) 8″ x 9″ construction paper
3. scissors and glue
4. crayons, paint, or paper scraps (for decorating)

Steps:

1. Fold both pieces of construction paper in two width-wise. Set the 6″ x 9″ paper aside.
2. Measure 2″ down from the top of the 8″ x 9″ paper and draw a line. Fold along the line and then open the page up and fold in two again.

3. Draw a triangle half way from the center fold to the line and cut away the extra paper. Open up the paper.

4. Fold the triangle down and draw around it. Lift up the triangle and fold up along the new lines on both sides.

5. Fold the center of the new diamond shape out so that when you fold the card the diamond will fold down and "pop out" when you open the card.

6. Glue the "pop out" card inside of the 6″ x 9″ paper, but do not put any glue behind the diamond. Decorate the card using the "pop out" for Santa Claus's hat, a Christmas Tree, or any other idea.

Hints:

The folding is very difficult for primary children.

MATCHING CARD AND PAPER

Materials:

1. (1) 4"x6" cardboard
2. string
3. tempera paint, any color and brush
4. glue and scissors
5. paper to print on such as tissue, butcher paper, newsprint, construction paper, any size

Steps:

1. Draw a simple design on the cardboard. Here are a few samples.

2. Squeeze glue onto the pencil lines and then put on the string. Press string down gently. Allow to dry thoroughly.
3. To print, paint string using the brush and tempera paint. Different parts of the design can be painted different colors. Turn and place in position on paper. Press down firmly on the cardboard with hand. Lift cardboard carefully. Several prints can be made with one printing.

Hints:

—Always use the same color paint on the string.
—Cards can be made of almost any kind of paper. Lighter weight paper makes the best wrapping paper.

January

SPONGE PAINTED SNOWMAN

Materials:

1. small pieces of sponge and clothespins
2. thick white tempera paint
3. scraps of paper, fabric, buttons and yarn
4. (1) 12"x18" light blue construction paper
5. scissors and paste or glue

Steps:

1. Clip clothespin to sponge and dip the sponge in white tempera paint. Sponge paint three connecting circles on the 12"x18" light blue construction paper. Paint on a bottom row of snow and snow falling.

 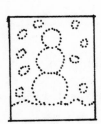

2. When the paint is dry, decorate the snowman with a scarf made of paper or fabric, button eyes, yarn scraps for the mouth and anything else desired. Use real small twigs for the arms.

Hints:

—Set up a table just for sponge painting. While some children are painting others can be making the clothes and decorations they will need for their snowman.

TORN PAPER SNOW PICTURES

Materials:

1. (1) 9"x12" blue or black construction paper
2. (1) 4½"x12" white construction paper
3. scraps of colored construction paper, all colors
4. paste or glue

Steps:

1. Tear the 4½"x12" white construction paper in half, lengthwise. Use one piece to make the ground. Tear the other piece into very small pieces for falling snow. Paste or glue the ground and some snowflakes on the blue or black paper.

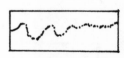
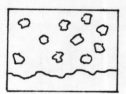

2. All other things in the picture must also be torn. They can be made from construction paper scraps of all colors. Make things from geometric shapes and piece them together. See illustrations below for some ideas:

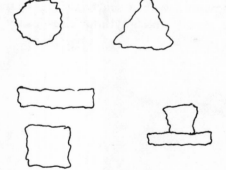

3. Add the rest of the torn pieces of white paper used for snow. The picture can also be sprayed with snow from a spray can.

SNOWFLAKE

Materials:

1. (1) 9"x9" square of tissue paper, any color
2. (1) 9"x9" square of white construction paper
3. scissors
4. liquid starch
5. paint brush
6. 6" piece of string or yarn

Steps:

1. Fold tissue paper as illustrated.

2. Cut off the corner points and then cut across at an angle. Cut out shapes on the folds and then open.

3. Cover the white construction paper with liquid starch, using the paint brush, and lay on the snowflake.

4. When the paper is dry, cut around the construction paper and staple yarn in a loop on one point or punch a hole to put the yarn through.

SNOWMAN MOBILE

Materials:

1. white construction paper squares:
   (4) 6"x6"   (4) 4"x4"   (4) 2"x2"
2. (4) 2"x3" pieces of colored construction paper
3. (2) 1"x6" pieces of colored construction paper (for arms)
4. (2) 2 ft. pieces of string
5. (4) pieces of black construction paper
6. scissors, glue or paste, black crayon

Steps:

1. Cut circles from the white construction paper squares. Cut hats from the 2"x3" pieces of colored construction paper. Cut out 2 at a time.

2. Lay out the circles and hat in order. Glue on arms. Run glue down the middle of the snowman and lay on the string.

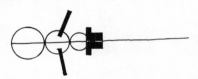

3. Cover the snowman with the second set of circles and hat. Draw faces and buttons.

4. Make two snowmen. Glue string to outside edges of the long strip. Glue the other strip over the string. Tie the strings together to hang.

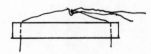

PENGUIN PUPPET

Materials:

1. (1) 9"x12" black construction paper
2. (1) 3"x4" white construction paper
3. (1) 1"x3" orange construction paper
4. (2) 3"x3" orange construction paper
5. (2) 3"x6" black construction paper
6. scissors and paste or glue

Steps:

1. Put paste along one 9" side of the 9"x12" black construction paper and roll into a tube. On the inside of the tube put paste about two inches around one end and pinch together. Round off corners.

2. Cut the 3"x6" pieces of black construction paper together, trimming off the corners to make wings. Paste to the back of the puppet. Fold the 3"x4" white construction paper in half and trim the corners to make the chest. Paste to the front.

3. Fold the two 3"x3" pieces of orange construction paper in half, together, and cut the webbed feet. Fold the top edge down about a half inch to make a tab and paste to the inside front edge of the puppet.

4. Fold the 1"x3" orange construction paper and round off the corners to make the beak. Make an additional fold, near the middle fold on each side, to provide a surface so it can be pasted to the body.

5. Use scraps of white and black construction paper to make the eyes.

SPRAY LEAF PATTERN

Materials:

1. (1) 9″x12″ black construction paper
2. a branch with small leaves on it
3. spray paint any color or a toothbrush and tempera paint
4. newspaper

Steps:

1. Select a small branch with small leaves on it or a pine branch. Place it on top of the black construction paper. Put newspaper under the black construction paper.

2. Spray the paper and branch with spray paint. The imprint underneath the leaves and branch will remain black. Another way to create the same effect is to dip an old toothbrush in tempera paint and then rub the thumb over the bristles, spraying the paint over the branch.

Hints:

—Use a few leaves on the black paper and spray with paint.
—Fold black paper and put design on half the paper. Use as a card or folder.

COVER YOUR SNEEZE

Materials:

1. (1) 9"x12" bright colored construction paper
2. (1) 7"x9" flesh colored construction paper
3. (1) 6"x6" flesh colored construction paper
4. (1) kleenex
5. (1) 4½"x6" brown or yellow construction paper
6. scissors, paste or glue and crayons

Steps:

1. Round off the corners of the 7"x9" flesh colored construction paper to make the face. Glue or paste onto the 9"x12" bright colored construction paper. Draw the facial features with crayons.

2. Trace around a hand on the 6"x6" flesh colored construction paper and cut out.

3. Cut the 4½"x6" brown or yellow paper into strips to make the hair. Paste or glue to head. Curl the ends of the strips by wrapping around a pencil.

4. Paste or glue the kleenex over the nose and place the hand over the kleenex.

VIOLET MOSAIC

Materials:

1. 2"x2" squares of light purple construction paper
2. 2"x2" squares of dark purple construction paper
3. scraps of yellow for flower centers
4. 2"x2" squares of green construction paper for leaves
5. green crayon
6. (1) 6"x12" white construction paper
7. scissors and glue or paste

Steps:

1. To make flower shapes cut into squares from each corner, almost to center. Cut off the corners.

2. Pinch sides of each petal together to make them three-dimensional. Glue bottom of flower to the white paper. Spread all over the paper.

 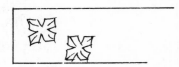

3. Paste yellow circles in flowers for centers. Cut out and paste on leaves.

4. Connect leaves and flowers together with the green crayon.

SURPRISE FLOWERS

Materials:

1. (1) 9″x12″ white construction paper
2. set of watercolors
3. soft bristle brush
4. container of water
5. small piece of sponge

Steps:

1. Wet paper completely on both sides. Dip sponge in water, wipe one side of paper, turn, smooth on desk, and make the other side wet.

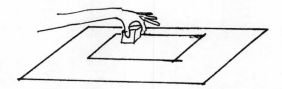

2. Fill brush with water and dip into paint. Get enough paint on brush to make a deep color.

3. Paint the flower shapes as a circle, blob or cross and watch the wet paper carry the paint out. Remember to put lines and blobs for leaves and stems.

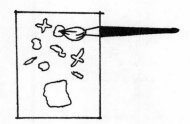   

4. When completely dry, draw the shapes of the flowers, leaves and vase with a black crayon.

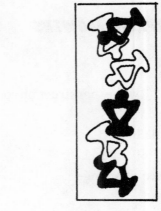

TISSUE PANEL

Materials:

1. (6) 5"x5" squares of colored tissue. 2 each of 3 colors
2. (1) 6"x18" white construction paper
3. scissors
4. liquid starch in small container
5. soft bristle brush

Steps:

1. Fold the tissue squares in half and cut out any design on the fold. It can be something like a butterfly, or a design. A part can also be cut from the center of the design to make it fancier. All pieces can be cut at the same time.

2. Arrange pieces on the white paper. Place them at different angles and have them overlap.

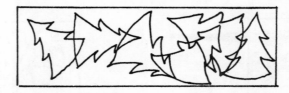

3. Put starch on paper and lay design pieces down carefully, one at a time. Put starch over each piece but be careful not to use too much starch or paint over the edge of the tissue as the color will run.

FOLD PRINTS

Materials:

1. 3 colors of thick tempera paint
2. paint brush, one for each color
3. (1) 9″x12″ piece of white paper

Steps:

1. Fold the 9″x12″ white paper in half.
2. Open the paper and dribble various colors of paint all over the paper.

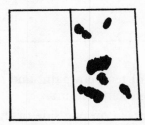

3. Fold the paper back up and smooth gently with hand.

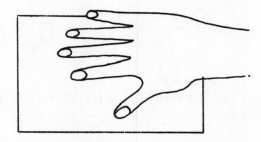

4. Open up and let dry. If mounting, you may have to stack something heavy on picture after dry to flatten.

Hints:

—These prints can be cut out and used as heads for imaginary animals. Make bodies of construction paper.

STRING PAINTING

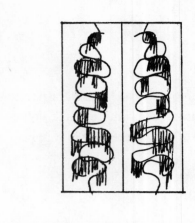

Materials:

1. 2 ft. piece of thin string
2. 2 colors of tempera paint, mixed very thin
3. (1) 12″x18″ white construction paper

Steps:

1. Fold the 12″x18″ white construction paper in half, lengthwise.

2. Dip the string in one color of tempera paint and squeeze off the excess paint by pulling between the first finger and thumb.
3. Lay the string in a wavy pattern on one side of the paper.

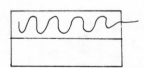

4. Fold over the paper and set one or two books on top. Carefully pull out the string with a swift pull.

BOOK

5. Open the design up and let it dry. Repeat again with another color of tempera paint on top of the same design.

CRAYON MOSAIC

Materials:

1. (1) 9"x12" graph paper with 1" squares
2. pencil
3. crayon

Steps:

1. Have the children draw a large object in the middle of the graph paper. (Examples: fruit, vegetables, geometric shapes.) Use the pencil and draw just the outline.

2. Discuss warm and cool colors. Have the children divide their crayons into two piles, warm and cool colors. (Cool: blue, green, purple; warm: orange, yellow, red)
3. Color the squares inside the design or shape either all warm colors or all cool colors. *Remind them not to put the same colors next to each other.*
4. Color the squares outside the shape in the opposite colors.

NAME DESIGNS

Materials:

1. 9″ x 12″ white or manila paper
2. crayons

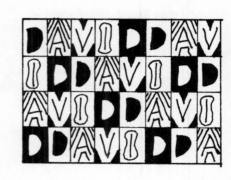

Steps:

1. Fold the 9″x12″ paper in half, widthwise....in half again....and then in half once more.

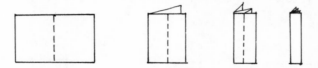

2. Open. Fold in half lengthwise and then in half again. Open, there will be 32 squares.

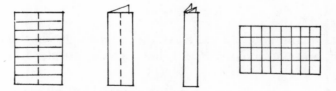

3. Flatten out paper. Write name, one letter in each box. Do over and over, moving from left to right, across the paper. Color in a design. Remember to do the same design with the same colors for each letter.

CRAYON FABRIC RUBBINGS

Materials:

1. small pieces of rough textured fabrics in any shape
2. old, peeled crayons
3. pastel colored newsprint or tissue paper, any color

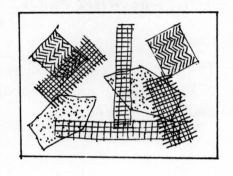

Steps:

1. Put one small piece of fabric under the paper to be used. Rub over it lightly with the side of the peeled crayon until the fabric texture appears. Rub over it harder to darken the color.

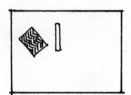

2. Put other pieces of fabric under the paper and repeat the process. Be sure to overlap the textures and use the same ones several times in different areas of the paper.

POSITIVE-NEGATIVE PANELS

Materials:

1. (1) 9"x12" white construction paper
2. (2 3"x9" black construction paper
3. scissors and paste or glue

Steps:

1. Fold the 9"x12" white construction paper in half, widthwise. Fold in half again. Open and lay flat.

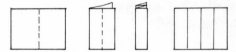

2. Fold the two 3"x9" pieces of black construction paper in half lengthwise, together. Cut out various shapes on the fold. Remember to leave a space between each shape and save all the pieces.

3. Paste or glue the two pieces of black construction paper to the white paper in alternate panels.

4. Match the small cutout pieces to the corresponding holes and glue or paste in the white panels.

Suggestions:

—Remind children to watch spacing and suggest the pieces be placed in order before pasting.
—These panels can be made with any two contrasting colors.

BLACK AND WHITE FACES

Materials:

1. (1) 9″x12″ white construction paper
2. (1) 6″ x 9″ black construction paper
3. scissors
4. paste or glue

Steps:

1. Fold the 9″x12″ white construction paper in half, widthwise. Slide the 6″x9″ black construction paper inside.

2. Draw half a face, with some kind of ear, on the white paper. Cut out. You will have a whole white face and half a black face.

3. Draw features on the black face: an eye, eyebrow, nose, mouth, and anything else desired. Cut these pieces out and paste or glue down what remains of the black face on half of the white face.

4. Paste or glue all the small pieces on the opposite side of the face.

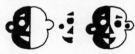

5. Use the black and white scraps to add personality to the face. Here are some suggestions:

BOX WEAVING

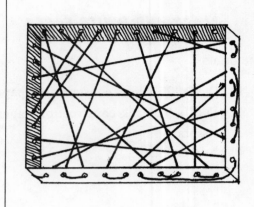

Materials:

1. a box lid with a narrow lip-shoe box, hosiery box, etc.
2. colored roving or rug yarn
3. hole punch or pointed tool to punch holes in box lid edge
4. large yarn needle or piece of small wire to use as a needle

Steps:

1. Punch holes around the entire edge of the box lid approximately ½ to ¾" apart.

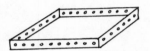

2. Using a length of roving or yarn which is not hard to handle (10 to 12') attach end of yarn through a hole and tie securely, knot to the inside. Thread yarn back and forth through holes. Many patterns and designs are possible.

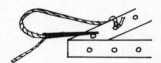

3. When one color is used start with a second color. Good choice of contrasting colors is essential for good design.

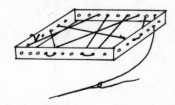

CIRCLE WEAVING

Materials:

1. (1) paper plate, any size
2. yarn, all colors and weights
3. scissors
4. needle or wire

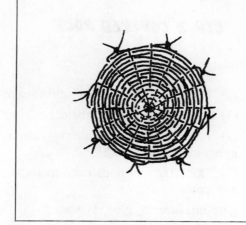

Steps:

1. Cut an uneven number of evenly spaced slits around the edge of the paper plate. Cut the slits so they point to the middle and are about ½″ long.

2. String paper plate for weaving by running a piece of yarn from one slit to the one directly across, through slit, under, and come up through the next slit. Remember to always cross the center.

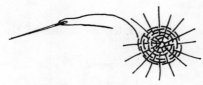

3. Start weaving in the center and weave round and round until the circle is as large as desired. To add other pieces of yarn, tie new piece to the end of the old with a knot.

4. To finish, cut the loops and tie 'neighbors' together. This is easier to do if the plate is turned over and only two loops at a time are cut. This will also free the weaving from the plate.

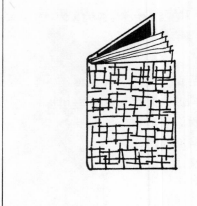

CLOTH COVERED BOOK

Materials:

1. (2) 6″x9″ cardboard or chipboard
2. (1) 11″x14½″ piece of fabric
3. (2) construction paper, any color, approximately 5½″x8½″
4. (2) 2″x9″ strips of construction paper, any color
5. glue mixture: ½ glue, ½ water
6. paint brush and stapler
7. 8½″x11″ pieces of paper for pages

Steps:

1. Brush the glue mixture on one side of each piece of cardboard. Press onto the material, leaving at least a 1″ border and a ½″ space between the pieces of cardboard.

2. Fold the corners of the fabric diagonally across the cardboard corners and glue down. Fold the borders of fabric over and glue to the cardboard.

3. Glue the 5½″x8½″ pieces of paper to the inside of the book, covering the edges of the fabric border.

4. Fold the 8½″x11″ pieces of paper in half and staple them together. There can be any number of pages. Insert the pages in the book by folding the 2″x9″ pieces of construction paper in half lengthwise, and gluing them on either side of the pages and cover.

February

PAPER MACHE HEX

Materials:

1. an oatmeal or salt box
2. (1) 18″ long dowel, ½″ thick
3. masking tape, scissors and glue
4. ½ cup of rice, beans or gravel
5. (3) 3″x5″ pieces of tagboard
6. newspaper torn in 1″ strips
7. wheat paste
8. tempera paint, various colors
9. yarn, buttons, feathers, ribbon

Steps:

1. In the center of the top and bottom of the box poke a hole with the scissors and insert the dowel. It should extend about 1″ above the top.

2. Tape the dowel to the bottom of the box securely with the masking tape. Remove the lid and add the rice, beans or gravel so that the hex will rattle. Put the lid back on and tape securely.

 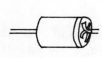

3. Use the three 3″ x 5″ pieces of tag for the nose. Mark the mid-point, 1½″, and draw lines from the corner to the point with a pencil. Cut and tape together to make a 3-D triangle. Tape to the box.

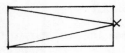 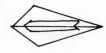

4. Apply several layers of paper mache, using newspaper and wheat paste over the box and nose. Let dry thoroughly.
5. Paint with the tempera paint and decorate with anything desired. It is advisable to give the hex a coat of fixative such as shellac, varnish, water-soluble gloss-medium before decorating.

PEOPLE CROWDS

Materials:

1. 2 pieces of black crayon
2. (1) 9"x12" white paper
3. watercolor paints
4. paint brush
5. container of water and a paper towel

Steps:

1. Put one crayon in each hand. Place the two crayons together at a point on the paper where the top of the head is to be. Drawing with both hands at the same time, not looking at the paper, *except when beginning a new figure,* draw as follows:

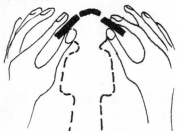

—around for the head and back together

—down for neck

—out for shoulders

—down for the arms

—around for the hands

—straight down to the edge of the paper

2. Repeat over and over, each time look and begin at a different level on the paper so the people are all different heights. Let them overlap. When the paper is full, go back over each figure with the crayon so the lines are very heavy.

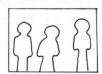 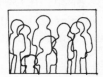

3. Paint the figures with watercolor paints. Paint those that appear to be in front one of the three primary colors; yellow. Paint the figures in the background with colors that are made with the primary color chosen. Such as yellow-orange, yellow-green, orange. Paint the background with one of the other two primary colors, blue or red.

NEWSPAPER CITIES

Materials:

1. (1) 9"x12" light blue construction paper
2. (1) piece of the classified section of the newspaper
3. small container of liquid starch
4. colored chalk
5. scissors and paint brush

Steps:

1. Cut buildings of all sizes and shapes from the piece of newspaper. (The classified section works best.)

2. Using the paint brush, cover the blue construction paper with liquid starch. Lay the buildings on, one at a time, and cover each with the liquid starch.

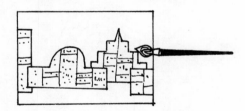

3. Give the entire picture one last coat of starch and then add details such as windows, chimneys, etc., with colored chalk.

Hints:

The chalk will adhere to the paper when it dries as the starch acts as a fixative but to be sure that none will rub off, the entire picture can be sprayed with chalk fixative or hair spray.

SILHOUETTE MOBILE

Materials:

1. (1) 9″ x 12″ black construction paper
2. (1) 6″ x 6″ light blue construction paper
3. scraps of red construction paper
4. paper punch
5. thread or string
6. scissors

Steps:

1. Trace, or cut out freehand, silhouettes of Lincoln and Washington, using the black construction paper.
2. Cut out hearts of all sizes by folding the pieces of red construction paper in half and drawing half a heart on the fold of each one.

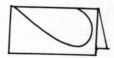

3. Cut out a circle spring from the light blue construction paper.

4. Tie the hearts and silhouettes to the string. Either punch holes and tie with string or use a needle and thread to sew the hearts to different points on the circle spring.

PATRIOTIC DESIGN

Materials:

1. squares of red, blue, and white construction paper (all sizes)
2. strips of red, blue, and white construction paper (all widths and lengths)
3. (1) 9″ x 12″ piece of manila paper
4. scissors and paste or glue

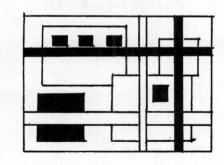

Steps:

1. Give each child a variety of squares and strips and one piece of 9″ x 12″ manila paper.
2. Have the children arrange the squares and strips in any design they wish. Encourage them to build out also. (See "Paper Building") Try many ways before pasting.

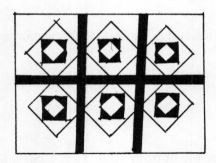 

3. After arranging, lift one piece at a time, apply paste or glue, and attach to paper.

PATRIOTIC SHIELD

Materials:

1. (1) 9″ x 12″ white construction paper
2. (1) 6″ x 6″ black construction paper
3. strips of red and blue construction paper (or paints of red and blue)
4. scissors and paste or glue

Steps:

1. Fold the 9″ x 12″ white construction paper in half, widthwise. Cut a shield shape as shown below.

2. Paste the red and blue strips on the shield to decorate. These can also be painted on with tempera or watercolors.

3. Fold the shield back in half and starting from the bottom, folded edge, cut loose a border 1″ from back edge to within 1″ of the top. Twist over top and glue point to the top, center point of the shield.

4. Cut a silhouette using the black paper. This can be cut freehand or from a pattern. Paste or glue to the center of the shield.

PATRIOTIC HAT

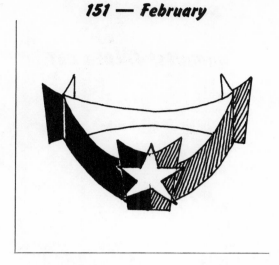

Materials:

1. (1) each 4½″ x 12″ red, white and blue construction paper
2. (1) 4″ x 4″ yellow construction paper
3. stapler
4. scissors and paste or glue

Steps:

1. Lay the red, white and blue strips of construction paper together and cut a curve from one end corner to the other, along one 12″ edge.

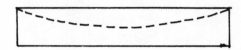

2. Staple the ends together, 2″ from corner, to make a three-corner hat. Fold back the 2″ edges at each corner.

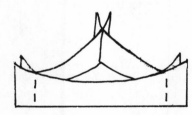
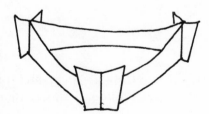

3. Cut a large star from the yellow paper and glue or paste it to one of the corners.

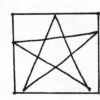
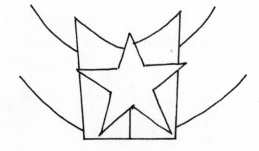

JAPANESE FOLDED HAT

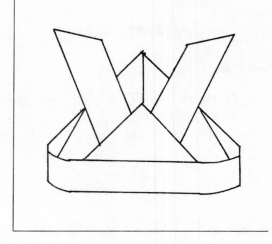

Materials:

1. one page of newspaper
2. stapler
3. crayons

Steps:

1. Fold one corner of the newspaper over the opposite edge. Cut off the extra strip. Keep it folded.

2. Fold the folded edge over two inches. Find the center and fold down the two corners.

3. Fold the two front pieces up and fold one of the two back pieces part way over the front. Leave it about 3″ lower than the middle line. Then fold this piece up.

4. Turn the hat over. Fold the single piece part way up and then fold the remaining 3″ up. Fold the corners over and staple on each side of the back of the hat.

5. Decorate the hat with crayons.

PATRIOTIC RESIST

Materials:

1. (1) 9″ x 12″ white construction paper
2. a white and black crayon
3. watercolor paints
4. paint brush
5. small container of water

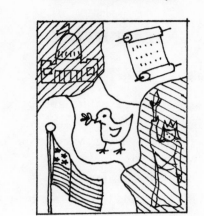

Steps:

1. Using the black crayon, divide the white paper into about five equal sections of various shapes.

2. Draw patriotic symbols in each section such as the flag, the statue of liberty, scroll, dove, eagle, capitol and the liberty bell with the white crayon. Press heavily.

3. Paint each section with a different color using the watercolor paints.

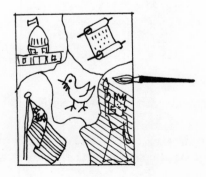

HEART MOBILE

Materials:

1. squares of red, white and pink construction paper; 3″, 4″, 5″
2. 5 pieces of string, varying in length from 6″ to 18″
3. scissors and paste or glue
4. odds and ends to decorate hearts
5. 12″ stick, reed, twig or wire

Steps:

1. Fold two construction paper squares in half, together, and cut half a heart. A simple way is to place the thumb at an angle on the fold and cut around the thumb. Cut the centers out of some to make heart rings. Make at least ten.

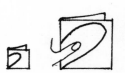

2. Paste or glue the hearts on the strings, placing the string between each pair of hearts. Stagger them at various intervals.

3. Decorate the hearts on both sides with odds and ends of paper, ribbon, yarn and fabric.
4. Tie the strings onto the stick, reed, twig or wire. Find the point on the stick where it will hang level and tie the string so the mobile can be hung.

VALENTINE DESIGN FOLDER

Materials:

1. (1) 12″ x 18″ white construction paper
2. (1) 9″ x 12″ red construction paper
3. scissors and paste or glue
4. a pencil
5. 24″ of red roving, yarn or string

Steps:

1. Fold the 9″ x 12″ red construction paper in half, widthwise. Draw on half a heart. Draw many inside of this. Cut out.

2. Arrange the heart rings on the 12″ x 18″ white construction paper. Try placing them in a row or scattering them all over the paper. Then paste or glue in the desired arrangement.

  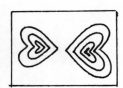

3. When the paste or glue is dry fold the 12″ x 18″ white construction paper in half, widthwise. Staple or paste the 9″ edges together. Punch a hole in each side and tie string to the folder.

VALENTINE BASKET

Materials:

1. (1) 6"x8" red construction paper
2. (1) 6"x18" white construction paper
3. (1) 1"x18" strip red construction paper
4. scissors and paste
5. any other materials you desire to decorate the valentine border

Steps:

1. Fold the red and white pieces of construction paper in half, widthwise. Hold together and round off the corners of the open ends.

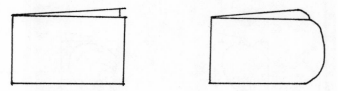

2. Lay open on the desk, one on top of the other, cross and fold back together. This will form the heart shape. Paste but be sure you do not paste it closed.

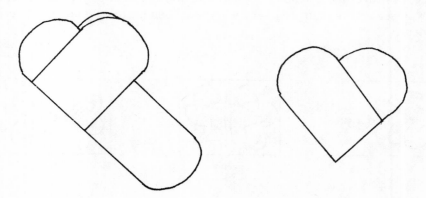

3. Paste or glue ends of handle to top of heart, in center.
4. Decorate with designs using crayons, tissue paper, scraps of construction paper, lace doilies or anything else.

HEART BUTTERFLY

Materials:

1. (2) 4½"x6" pieces of white construction paper
2. (1) 3"x6" piece of red construction paper
3. pipe cleaner
4. scissors and paste
5. pencils

Steps:

1. Fold one 4½"x6" piece of white construction paper in half, lengthwise. Draw on half a heart and cut out.

2. Fold the other piece of 4½"x6" white construction paper, trace half of the other heart and cut out. This will make two hearts of the same size.
3. From scraps, cut out a red heart for the body and two little hearts for the top of the feelers.
4. Cut two narrow white pieces for feelers.
5. Paste or glue the pieces together.

6. Attach a pipe cleaner to the underside of the butterfly. Then the butterfly can be made to appear to fly on bulletin boards, chairs, etc.

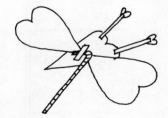

VALENTINE CARD

Materials:

1. (1) 9″x12″ white construction paper
2. (1) 6″x9″ red construction paper
3. scissors and paste or glue
4. pencil

Steps:

1. Fold the 6″x9″ piece of red construction paper in half and draw on a valentine heart pattern.

2. Cut out. Cut small hearts or pieces from the center of the design. Save.
3. Fold the 9″x12″ piece of white construction paper in half, lengthwise. Paste the heart design on the front.

4. Open the card and paste the center hearts on the inside of the cover. The valentine message can go on the right hand side.

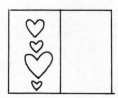

HEART OF MESSAGES

Materials:

1. (1) 9″x12″ red construction paper
2. (1) 6″x6″ white construction paper
3. 1 brad
4. scraps of all kinds for decorating
5. scissors and paste or glue

Steps:

1. Fold on 9″x12″ red construction paper in half in either direction and cut out half a heart. Cut a window on the fold in the top part of the heart.

2. Fold the 6″x6″ white construction paper in half and round off the open corners to make a circle.

3. Place the white circle behind the red heart, placing it so it does not show from the front. Push the brad through the middles of the heart and white circle, folding the prongs back on the white circle.

4. Write a message in the window, turn the circle and write another message. Keep going until the spaces are used up.

5. Decorate the heart with the scraps of all kinds of material.

CARDBOARD PRINTING

Materials:

For stamp:

    1. a square of heavy cardboard

    2. scraps of cardboard

    3. white glue and scissors

For printing:

    1. paper to print on, any kind

    2. thick tempera paint, any color

    3. paint brush

Steps:

1. Using the scraps of cardboard, cut out shapes to be printed and glue them to the square of cardboard. For added effect, lines and texture can be scratched into the cardboard with a pointed object. Letters and words should be a mirror image.

2. To print use the paint brush to apply tempera paint to the designs glued onto the cardboard. Turn over and press down firmly on paper to be printed. Make a practice print before printing on selected paper.

3. Carefully place the stamp face down on the paper and press gently on the top. Lift and print again. It is possible to get two or three prints from one painting.

Suggestions:

—Print on any kind of paper, such as tissue, butcher, newspaper, construction paper, paper towels, newsprint. Very nice textures can be achieved when using rough paper.

SHADOW BOX VALENTINES

Materials:

1. box lids, not more than 1″ deep
2. scraps of all kinds of paper, different colors and textures
3. scraps of yarn, string, ribbon
4. glue and scissors
5. paper doilies

Steps:

1. Cut the paper doilies in half and glue them all around the edge of the inside of the box to make a frame for the shadow box.

2. Using various kinds of paper make a background on the bottom of the box. Before adding details write a message with yarn, paper or anything else.

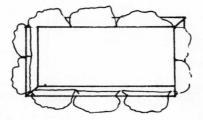

3. Add any sort of details desired such as pop-out hearts, springs, pictures and other verses. Things can be hung in the box with string or thread.

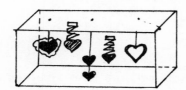

TRANSPARENT TISSUE DESIGN

Materials:

1. (2) wax paper, same size
2. small pieces of tissue paper, many colors
3. glue mixture; ½ glue, ½ water
4. paint brush and scissors
5. newspaper
6. iron

Steps:

1. Cut various shapes from the tissue paper pieces such as hearts, flowers, snow-flakes, leaves or geometric designs. Cut more than one at a time so the various shapes will be repeated.

2. Place one piece of wax paper on a sheet of newspaper. Paint the wax paper with a coat of the glue mixture. Arrange the tissue paper shapes one at a time, and cover with glue mixture. Place the second sheet of wax paper on top.

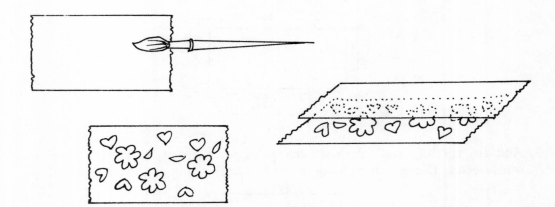

3. Place the waxpaper layers between newspapers and iron, using a warm iron.

NAME CONTOUR LINE DESIGN

Materials:

1. (1) 9″x12″ white or manila paper
2. crayons

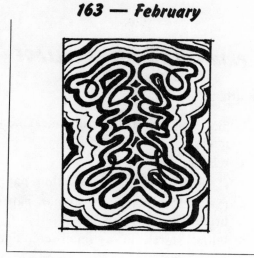

Steps:

1. Fold the white paper in half, lengthwise. Open and lay flat on the desk. Write the name on the fold line with a black crayon.

2. Fold the paper back up and rub across it with a hand very hard. This will transfer the name to the other side in reverse.

3. Go around the name with a bright colored contour line. Follow the curves in the name. Keep going around, again and again, each time with a different colored crayon. Make some lines thicker than others and some farther apart.

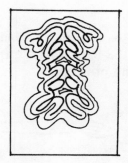

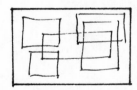

PRINTING ON TISSUE COLLAGE

Materials:

1. pieces of styrofoam from meat containers
2. scissors
3. (1) 9"x12" white construction paper
4. (5) 5"x5" squares of tissue paper, bright colors
5. liquid starch in a small container
6. paint brush
7. India ink or black tempera paint

Steps:

1. Paint the white construction paper with a coat of liquid starch. Lay the squares of tissue paper on the white paper, one at a time, covering each with a coat of starch. Let them overlap to make a more interesting design.

2. While the background is drying cut the pieces of styrofoam into shapes desired.

3. Paint the pieces of styrofoam with the India ink or black tempera paint. Place each face down on the background paper in the area desired and press gently. Pick up carefully and print again.

WEAVING PLASTIC TRAYS

Materials:

1. plastic or styrofoam meat tray, any size
2. scissors, pencil, ruler
3. thin black or white string or thread, lots
4. single-edged razor or mat knife
5. large-eyed needle
6. yarns and strings, light and medium weight
7. newsprint and masking tape

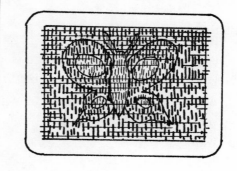

Steps:

1. Make the loom by cutting out the center section of the meat tray with the razor or mat knife. Follow the lines on the tray. Don't cut on the sides.

2. Make dots ¼″ apart at each end of the tray.

3. Thread the needle with a long piece of the black or white string or thread and knot the end. Sew across the loom from one dot to the dot across. Pull the string taut, but not so tight as to pull the frame out of shape.

4. Weave a design with the colored yarns and strings. A design can be planned on newsprint and taped behind the loom with masking tape.

MARBLED CHALK

Materials:

1. colored chalk
2. large flat pan, square or rectangle
3. white paper, size depending on pan
4. scraping object
5. water

Steps:

1. Fill the large flat pan with water.
2. Scrape various colors of chalk onto the surface of the water. The chalk will float on the top of the water.

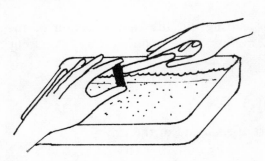

3. Place the white paper on the top of the water and chalk. Lightly touch the paper to be sure the chalk is picked up.

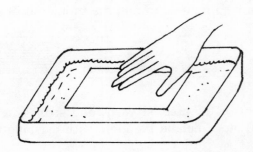

4. Life the paper out carefully and lay flat on a newspaper to dry.

SCRAPED PAINTING

Materials:

1. (1) 9″x12″ white construction paper
2. tempera paint in squeeze bottles; at least three colors
3. (1) 3″x10″ stiff cardboard strip (one for each painting to be made)
4. newspapers to cover working surface

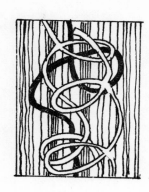

Steps:

1. Place the 9″x12″ white construction paper on newspaper to protect working surface.
2. Squeeze three colors of tempera paint onto the white paper in 'squiggelly' lines and dribbles.

3. Hold the cardboard strip at one end of the paper. Hold the paper with the other hand. Firmly scrape the paint off *with one stroke only* without lifting the cardboard edge off the paper.

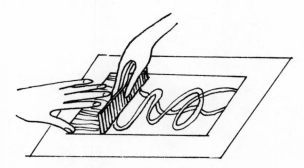

Hint :

— Use the cardboard scraper only once. Be sure to scrape the paint sideways so it doesn't end up all over the place.

March

169

LEPRECHAUN

Materials:

1. (1) 9"x12" white construction paper
2. (2) 6"x9" green construction paper
3. crayons
4. orange yarn
5. scissors and glue or paste

Steps:

1. Draw a face at the top of the 9"x12" white construction paper, giving it pointed ears. Make the head about 3" wide and 2" high.

2. Fold one 6"x9" green construction paper in half, widthwise, and cut out the pants. Fold the other 3"x9" green construction paper in half, widthwise, and cut the parts for the jacket as illustrated. Make a hat and two collars with the scraps.

  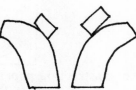

3. Paste or glue the clothes on the white paper. Add the orange yarn for hair and a beard. Use construction paper scraps or crayons to add anything else desired such as shoes, hands and a pipe.

POTATO PEOPLE

Materials:

1. (2) 6"x9" brown construction paper
2. (1) 6"x9" black construction paper
3. (8) 3"x9" squares of green construction paper
4. (1) 4½"x6" green construction paper
5. scissors and paste or glue
6. crayons
7. scraps of yellow construction paper for eyes

Steps:

1. Draw potato shapes on the brown construction paper for the heads and cut out.

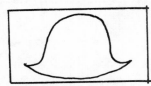

2. Draw a hat shape on the black construction paper and cut out.

3. Using green construction paper, cut out clovers.

4. Make the eyes from scraps and paste the potato people together.

5. Crayons can be used to add detail.

PULL APART SHAMROCK

Materials:

1. (1) 9"x12" green construction paper
2. (1) 9"x12" white construction paper or any other color for background
3. a pencil
4. scissors and paste or glue

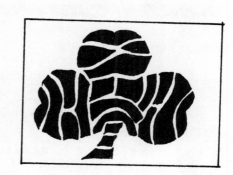

Steps:

1. Fold the 9"x12" green construction paper in half, widthwise, and draw on a shamrock. A simple way is to draw three circles and a stem. Cut it out.

2. Cut the shamrock into many pieces, like a puzzle. Place each piece on the desk making sure they do not get out of order or it will be almost impossible to put back together.

3. Arrange the pieces of the shamrock on the white construction paper, placing them so that there are spaces between each piece. When all are in place then lift one at a time and glue or paste to the white paper.

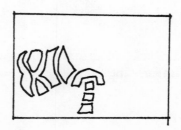

FINGERPAINT CLOVER FIELD

Materials:

1. (1) piece of fingerpaint, butcher or shelf paper
2. green tempera paint mixed with liquid starch, very thick
3. 3"x3" pieces of tissue paper in shades of green or bright colors
4. scissors and newspapers

Steps:

1. Place several 3"x3" squares of tissue paper together and cut out shamrocks. Make them many different sizes. A simple way to make shamrocks is to draw three circles and a stem.

2. Place the background paper on a piece of newspaper. Pour about 3 tablespoons of the thick tempera paint in the middle and spread all over the paper with one hand. Make an all-over fingerpaint design on the paper.
3. Before the fingerpainting dries, place the tissue shamrocks in position all over the fingerpaint design.

Suggestions:

—If you wish, make the shamrocks of green tissue paper, and use several colors of tempera paint for the fingerpainting.

STRING STAMPS

Materials:

1. 4½"x6" piece heavy cardboard
2. pieces of heavy yarn
3. strong, white glue
4. pencil

Materials:

1. construction paper, any size
2. paint brush
3. tempera paint
4. water

Steps:

1. Draw free form design on cardboard with pencil.
2. Put glue on the pencil lines.
3. Glue yarn on the line. Let dry before printing.

Steps:

1. Paint string on stamp. Parts can be painted different colors.
2. Lay the stamp face down very carefully on the construction paper and press gently. (You should get about 3 prints before you have to repaint. Use the same colors when repainting)

ANIMALS IN CAGES

Materials:

1. (1) shoe box
2. (1) 6"x9" construction paper color or animal to be made
3. (5-6) ½"x9" black construction paper strips
4. yarn, buttons, scraps of fabric
5. construction paper scraps
6. scissors and paste or glue

Steps:

1. Cut out any animal desired from the 6"x9" construction paper. Make the legs extra long so part can be folded back. Decorate the animal with yarn, buttons scraps of fabric or construction paper and crayons.

2. Decorate the inside of the shoe box with scraps of paper, fabric and crayons to look like the inside of a zoo cage. Remember that the open top of the box will become the side of the cage. Fold back part of the animals legs and paste or glue to the bottom of the inside of the cage. Add a supporting strip behind his head and attach to the back of the box.

3. Fold the ends of the ½"x9" black construction paper strips so they are the width of the box and then glue or paste across the front of the cage. Space as evenly as possible.

4. The outside of the box can be painted or covered with paper or fabric if desired.

3-PERSON SILLY ANIMALS

Materials:

1. (1) 9″x12″ white drawing paper
2. crayons
3. lots of imagination

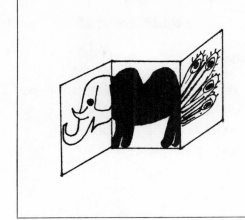

Steps:

1. Divide the children into groups of three.
2. Fold the 9″x12″ white drawing paper into three equal sections, widthwise.

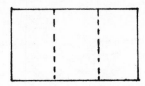

3. Open the paper flat. Starting from the left, the first person draws the head of an animal, any type of animal, on the first section only, stopping at the fold.

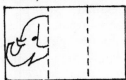

4. The first section is folded back and the paper is passed to the second person. The next person draws the body of an animal, stopping at the second fold.

5. The second section is then folded back and passed to the third person. The third person adds a tail section without knowing one thing about the other two sections.

FUZZY ANIMAL

Materials:

1. (1) 9"x12" white construction paper
2. (1) piece of sponge
3. water in a small container
4. watercolor paints and brush

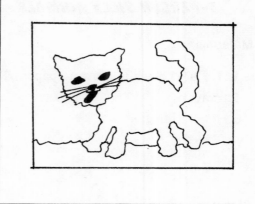

Steps:

1. Dip sponge in water and wet both sides of the paper. Make one side wet, turn over and stretch tightly on the desk so there are no wrinkles. Then make the top side wet.

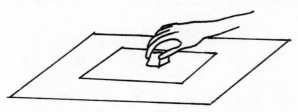

2. Decide what fur animal will be made such as a cat, bear, dog, or llama. Fill brush with paint of chosen color and paint the outline of the animal on quickly. Don't try to do it perfectly. While the paper is still wet fill in the animal's face and body. Leave a white spot where the eye will go. Let dry.

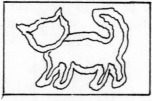

3. When the painting is dry, add eyes, whiskers, tongue and background with watercolor paints or crayons.

ROLLED BIRDS

Materials:

1. 1"x12" strips of construction paper, any color desired
2. (1) 9"x12" pastel color construction paper for background
3. scissors and paste or glue
4. scraps of construction paper

Steps:

1. Paste ends of one 1"x12" strip together to make the shape of the body. Cut one piece in half and make two circles. Use one for the head and pinch one end of the other to make the wing. Arrange these on the pastel construction paper to form a bird. Put paste on edges and attach to paper.

 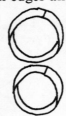 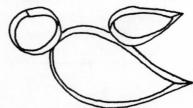

2. Roll the 1"x12" strips into coils and paste the ends. Make some tight and some loose. Do enough to fill the shape of the bird. Put them in the shape to test.

3. Take out the coils, put paste or glue on the edge and side of each coil and put back in the shape. Add eyes, a beak and feet with scraps.

Suggestions:

—These birds can be made into a mobile.
—Make like the fruit in the November section.

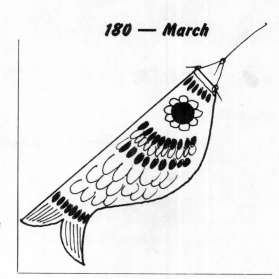

NEWSPAPER CARP KITE

Materials:

1. 1 full sheet of newspaper, classified section — 28"x22"
2. pencil, scissors, paste or glue
3. newspaper for stuffing
4. light-weight wire or string for inside of mouth
5. masking tape
6. chalk, crayons or paint to decorate

Steps:

1. Discuss fish: shape, color, design (pattern of gills, scales, etc.) Look at pictures of all kinds of fish.

2. Fold the newspaper in half lengthwise. Design and draw a fish form. The back of the fish must be on the folded edge. Cut out the fish shape: do not cut along the fold at the top.

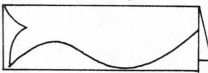 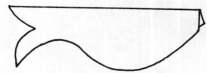

3. Open the fish shape and lay it flat. Using paint, chalk or crayons, make designs on the fish.

4. To strengthen the mouth edge, fold back the paper about ½" twice and glue down. Tape wire or string the length of the mouth.

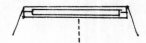

5. Fold the fish back together and glue the edges. Stuff with crinkled up newspaper, either before or after gluing edges closed.

6. To hang: Attach wire or string to the edges of the mouth.

WINDMILL

Materials:

1. (1) 9"x9" butcher, shelf or construction paper, any color
2. crayons
3. paper punch
4. (1) tack or small nail
5. (1) stick; twig or ¼" dowling

Steps:

1. Fold the 9"x9" square of paper in half, diagonally, from one corner to the other. Open. Fold in half diagonally in the opposite direction. Open and cut.

 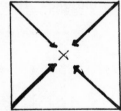

2. Punch a hole in one corner of each piece (same place in each section) and one hole in the middle. If desired, draw designs on the paper with crayons.

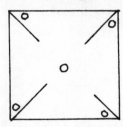

3. Fold over each corner with a hole in it to the middle, put a tack or small nail through the holes and attach to the stick.

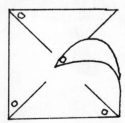

TISSUE KITES

Materials:

1. (2) 9″x12″ or 12″x18″ colored construction paper for kite
2. pieces of tissue paper, all colors
3. string, roving or yarn
4. scissors, pencil, paste or glue

Steps:

1. Fold the two pieces of construction paper together in half, lengthwise. Then fold in half, widthwise. Hold the corner with all the folds and cut diagonally across the paper, from one corner to the other to make the kite shape. Leave folded.

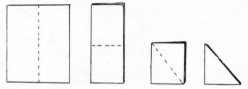

2. Draw a ½″ border along the open edge. Cut shapes along both folded edges and cut out as illustrated. This will make two kite shapes.

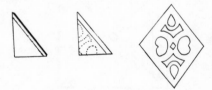

3. Fill the open spaces of one kite with tissue. Lay a piece of tissue under the space to be filled and draw around it with a pencil. Cut out tissue, leaving a small border and paste to kite. When all spaces are filled paste other kite on top to cover tissue paper edges. Add a tail to the kite with string and tissue paper.

LITTER EATER

Materials:

1. (1) ½ gallon milk carton
2. (2) cup sections from egg carton
3. white construction paper
   (1) 8″x15″ (1) 5″x5″ (4) 2″x6″
4. (1) 2″x3″ red construction paper
5. (3) 3″x6″ black construction paper
6. (1) 12″ piece of yarn or roving
7. scissors and glue

Steps:

1. Cut the top off the milk carton and slant down the sides about 2″ with scissors.

2. Cover the milk carton with the 8″x15″ white paper. Trim the sides to match the slants. Make the lid from the 5″x5″ white paper. Fold the edges back about 1″ and cut the mouth as illustrated. Trim off the corners.

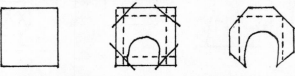

3. Tie the ends of the yarn together. Place it behind the back fold of the lid. Glue the lid to the carton, placing it between the paper and the carton sides.

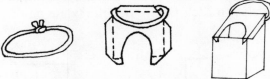

4. Trim the egg carton cups and glue to the lid for eyes.

5. Cut ears and eyes from the black paper; and legs from the white paper. Fold tabs on the end of each piece and glue them to the carton.

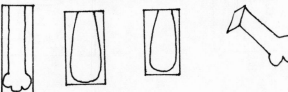

PUSSY WILLOWS

Materials:

1. (1) 12"x18" construction paper any pastel color
2. (1) 6"x9" construction paper, any color, for vase
3. brown crayon and scissors
4. thick gray and white tempera paint
5. scissors and paste or glue

Steps:

1. On the 12"x18" pastel colored construction paper, draw stems for the pussy willows with the brown crayon. If they are to be in a vase first fold the 6"x9" piece of construction paper in half and cut out a vase. Paste vase on the paper and draw the stems coming out of the vase. Decorate the vase with crayons.

2. Put small amounts of the gray and white tempera paint on wax paper or in small containers. Dip a fingertip in the gray paint and print pussies on the stem. Add white tips to each pussy with the white paint.

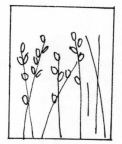 

CLOWNS

Materials:

1. (1) 12"x18" pastel color construction paper
2. (1) 3"x3" skin color construction paper
3. scraps of paper, fabric, ribbon, yarn and buttons
4. scissors and paste or glue
5. crayons

Steps:

1. Fold the 3"x3" skin color construction paper in half and trim off the open corners to make a circle for the face. Attach this to the 12"x18" pastel color paper in the center, near the top.

2. Cut the scraps of fabric into strips about two inches wide to make the clothes. Piece the pants and shirt parts and glue or paste to paper.

3. Add facial features, shoes, hands, toys and so forth with the scraps of fabric, paper, yarn, ribbon and buttons.

Hints:

—Before beginning the project, have a child spray the scraps of fabric with spray starch and then iron flat. This gives the fabric some body and makes it easier to cut.

INSECT PUPPETS

Insect Puppets

Materials:

1. paper bag — size #5
2. (1) 6"x9" color construction paper for the body
3. (1) 4½"x6" construction paper for head
4. (1) 9"x12" construction paper for wings
5. (8) 1"x8" construction paper for legs
6. (2) 1"x12" construction paper for antennae
7. scissors and paste or glue
8. crayons and scraps of paper for details

Steps:

1. Fold 9"x12" pieces of construction paper in half and draw on shapes for body, head and wings.

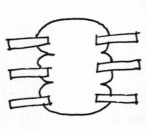

2. Paste the legs on the back side of the body piece. Attach with paste to paper sack. Also add head and wings.

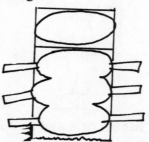 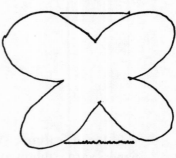

3. Paste antennae behind wings. Add details with crayons and scraps.

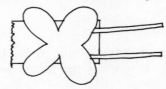

BURLAP FLOWERS

Materials:

1. scraps of burlap, all colors
2. large eyed needle
3. scissors
4. yarn of various colors, light and medium weights

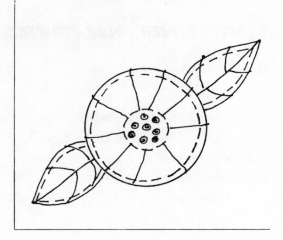

Steps:

1. Cut round circles at least 4″ in diameter from the burlap, for the flowers. Cut any shape for the leaves, remembering to leave enough fabric so an edge can be turned under.

2. Turn the edges under on the flower and leaves. Using a running stitch, hem the edges of the flower and leaves with yarn.

3. Using any stitches desired, decorate the flower and leaves.

4. When the flowers are completed, they can be glued or stitched to construction paper or to a piece of burlap to make a wall hanging.

UNCONTROLLED COLOR FLOWERS

Materials:

1. watercolors
2. brushes, large and small
3. (1) 9"x12" white drawing paper
4. water container and paper towels
5. small sponge, 2"x2"
6. a black crayon or felt tip pen

Steps:

1. Fill the sponge with water. Using even strokes, wet one side of the paper. Turn paper over and flatten out on the surface of the desk. Make sure it is smooth. Make the top side wet.

2. Using the sponge filled with water, make the bottom third of the paper wet. With a brush, outline the shape of a vase and drop color into it.

3. Make the rest of the paper wet. Drop colors for flowers and leaves where desired. Let the colors meet and fuse. Use colors that will bleed well together. Allow to dry.

4. To finish, use black crayon or a felt tip pen and outline flower shapes, leaves and vase.

TISSUE BUTTERFLIES

Materials:

1. (1) 9"x12" construction paper, any color
2. (1) 9"x12" newsprint
3. 2"x2" squares of tissue paper, all colors
4. (1) 3"x6" black construction paper
5. scissors and paste or glue

Steps:

1. Fold the 9"x12" newsprint in half, widthwise, and draw on the shape of a butterfly. Cut out. Open and place in the center of the 9"x12" construction paper. Trace around it.

2. Fold the black construction paper in half, lengthwise, and cut out the butterfly's body shape. Cut antennae from the scraps. Paste or glue to the outline of the butterfly on the construction paper.

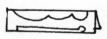 

3. Put a small dot of paste or glue on the butterfly's wing. On this drop a tissue paper square and pinch up the sides. Repeat this until all of the butterfly is covered. The tissue squares can also be wrapped around the end of a pencil and then dipped in paste or glue and pushed onto the wing. Use lots of colors and create matching patterns on each wing.

 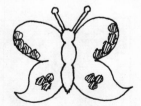 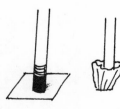

TISSUE DESIGNS

Materials:

1. (1) 12"x18" grey bogus paper
2. (10) 4"x4" squares of three different colors of tissue paper
3. small container of liquid starch
4. paint brush
5. paint brush
6. scissors
7. black crayon

Steps:

1. Fold the 4"x4" tissue squares in half. Do several at one time. Cut different shapes on the fold.

2. Using the paint brush, apply liquid starch to the grey bogus paper. Lay tissue shapes on, covering each with liquid starch. Remember to overlap the shapes.

3. When dry, outline the shapes with black crayon.

HAPPY SUN FACES

Materials:

1. (1) 9″x12″ white construction paper
2. shades of yellow crayons
3. orange watercolor paint
4. small container of water
5. paint brush

Steps:

1. Draw happy, smiling faces with the various shades of yellow crayons all over the 9″x12″ white construction paper. Make them all sizes and shapes. Fill the whole paper. Color very heavily.

2. Paint a wash over the entire picture with the orange watercolor paint. Use a wide brush and go over the picture only once. Painting over and over the drawing will break down the wax and the faces will not show through the wash.

April

EASTER MOBILE

Materials:

1. (1) 6"x18" green construction paper
2. (1) each 3"x8" white, light blue, pink, light green and yellow construction paper
3. pieces of heavy yarn in the same colors as the construction paper
4. scissors and paste or glue
5. crayons

1. Fold the green construction paper, lengthwise. Cut a wavy line edge along one edge.

2. Fold the 3"x8" pieces of construction paper in half and cut out Easter things; bunnies, chickens, eggs, flowers, etc. Leave bottom edge on the fold.

3. Put paste all over one side of each object. Lay one end of the yarn near the top of the object and then fold over and paste closed.

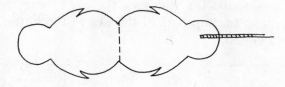

4. Open up the green construction paper and put on a line of paste. Space the ends of the yarn inside and close up. Hold together until the paste dries. Color designs and faces on the cut out objects.

CHICKEN IN THE EGG

Materials:

1. (1) 9"x12" white construction paper
2. (1) 6"x9" yellow construction paper
3. (1) 12"x18" colored construction paper
4. scraps of construction paper, in many colors
5. a brad
6. scissors and paste or glue

Steps:

1. Fold the white construction paper in half, lengthwise. Hold the fold and cut the corners on the open edges to make an egg shape.

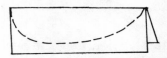 

2. Fold the yellow construction paper in half, lengthwise. Cut half a chick shape, holding the fold. You may wish to draw this with a pencil first.

3. Using the scraps of colored construction paper cut any kind of shapes such as circles, squares, rings, triangles, flowers, butterflies, etc., to decorate egg. Paste all over the egg. Make sure they are well pasted.

4. Cut a zig-zag line across the width of the egg. Paste the chicken behind the bottom part. Attach the top part of the egg to the bottom with the brad so it swings open and closed.

 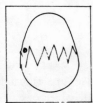 

PAPER MACHE EGG

Materials:

1. (1) balloon
2. newspapers and paper towels
3. liquid starch
4. many 5"x5" squares of tissue paper, all colors
5. paint brush and scissors

Steps:

1. Blow up balloon and tie end. Tear tissue squares into small shapes.
2. Apply several layers of the tissue shapes to the surface of the balloon with liquid starch. Paint balloon with starch and lay on pieces of tissue. Cover each piece with starch.

3. Apply two layers of torn pieces of newspaper, covering the first layer of tissue paper with liquid starch. Use narrow strips or circular shape pieces of torn newspaper. Put one layer of torn pieces of paper towel over the newspaper.

4. To decorate the outside of the egg, put another layer of tissue paper shapes with liquid starch. Let dry.
5. Cut a hole in the paper mache egg with scissors. Fill with green paper grass and put in Easter eggs, cut out ducks and rabbits or anything else desired.

BUNNY

Materials:

1. (1) 12"x18" white construction paper
2. cotton
3. crayons
4. scissors and paste or glue

Steps:

1. Fold white paper in half, lengthwise. Draw an outline of the bunny as seen from the side. Cut it out.

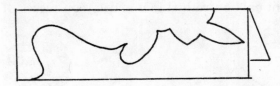

2. Paste the hands together and paste cotton on for the tail. Color the inside of the ears and draw on face and paws.

RABBIT PUPPET

Materials:

1. white construction paper cut to the following sizes:
   - (1) 9"x12"
   - (2) 3"x9"
   - (2) 3"x6"
   - (2) 3"x4"
2. (2) 2"x8" pink construction paper
3. scraps of construction paper: orange, green, blue, black
4. scissors and paste or glue

Steps:

1. Put paste on one 9" edge of the 9"x12" white construction paper and roll into a tube. Put paste all the way around the inside, about two inches down, on one end of the tube and pinch together to make top. Round off the corners.

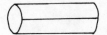 

2. Fold the two 3"x9" pieces of white construction paper in half, lengthwise, and trim off one corner to make ears. Do the same to the two 2"x8" pieces of pink paper. Paste or glue the pink inside the white.

3. Place the two 3"x6" pieces of white construction paper together and round the corners of one end to make the arms. Paste or glue to the back of the tube, in the middle. Also put on the ears.

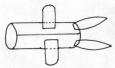

4. Fold the two 3"x4" pieces of white paper, widthwise, and cut the feet. Fold the straight edge back ½" to make a tab and attach to the inside front of the tube with paste or glue.

5. Add eyes, nose, mouth, carrot or basket and whiskers cut from the construction paper scraps.

BUNNY MASK

Materials:

1. (1) 10"x10" white construction paper
2. (2) 3"x9" white construction paper
3. (2) 2"x9" pink construction paper
4. (1) 2"x2" pink construction paper
5. (2) 2"x2" light blue construction paper
6. (2) 1"x1" black construction paper
7. narrow strips of white construction paper for whiskers
8. scissors and paste or glue

Steps:

1. Fold the 10"x10" white construction paper in half and trim the corners on the open edges to make a circle.

2. Fold the 3"x9" white strips and the 2"x9" pink strips in half, lengthwise. Trim the corners on one end to make the pointed ears. Paste the pink inside of the white construction paper.

3. Trim the corners of the pink, blue and black construction paper squares. Paste the black circles on the blue for eyes.

4. Open the circle and lay flat on the desk. In the very center put paste, lay on whiskers and then the pink nose. Paste on the eyes and ears. Cut up the fold almost to the nose. Pull one edge over the other and paste or staple so the mask will curve around the face.

BUNNY BASKET

Materials:

1. (1) ½ gallon milk carton
2. (1) 4″x18″ pink construction paper
3. (2) 4″x10″ pink construction paper
4. (1) 2″x18″ pink construction paper
5. scissors and white glue
6. cotton

Steps:

1. Using scissors, cut the milk carton down so it is about four inches high. Glue the 4″x18″ pink construction paper around the milk carton. Trim off any excess paper.

2. Glue the 2″x18″ strip of pink construction paper to the sides of the milk carton to make the handle.

3. Fold the two 4″x10″ pieces of construction paper in half together, lengthwise, and cut out half a bunny shape. Open.

4. Glue the bunny shapes to the covered milk carton, one on each side. Use the cotton to make tails.

DUCK PUPPETS

Materials:

1. (1) 9" x 12" yellow construction paper
2. (2) 3" x 3" orange construction paper
3. (2) 3" x 6" yellow construction paper
4. (1) 2" x 4" orange construction paper
5. black crayon
6. scissors and paste or glue

Steps:

1. Paste one 9" edge of the 9" x 12" yellow construction paper and roll into a tube. Hold firmly until set. On the inside of the tube put paste about two inches down and pinch the top together. Round off the corners of the top.

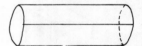

2. Cut the 3" x 6" yellow construction paper into wings. Cut both at the same time. Paste to the tube, in the middle of the back.

3. Fold and cut the 3" x 3" orange construction paper into webbed feet. Fold the top part of the feet down about one inch, paste and attach to the body.

4. Fold the 2" x 4" orange construction paper and round the open edge corners. Fold again to make a flat surface and paste onto the duck.

5. Color in the eyes with a black crayon.

PAPER SACK DUCK

Materials:

1. (1) yellow paper sack, #5
2. piece of string
3. 1½ sheets of newspaper
4. orange construction paper: (2) 3″ x 4″
   (2) 2″ x 4″
5. scraps of black construction paper
6. scissors and paste or glue

Steps:

1. Wrinkle and wad up the two pieces of newspaper into two balls.
2. Put the largest newspaper ball in the bottom of the paper sack and tie the string around the bag just about the ball. Put the smaller newspaper ball in the sack and fold the top of the bag over the top and paste or glue down.

3. Trim off the corners of the two 3″ x 6″ pieces of yellow construction paper for the wings. Fold the two 3″ x 4″ pieces of orange construction paper together, length-wise, and cut the feet. Paste or glue feet and wings to the body.

4. Round off the corners of the 2″ x 4″ piece of orange construction paper and fold so it has a flat surface to paste or glue to the head for the beak. Cut eyes from the black paper scraps and paste on head.

EGG CARTON FLOWERS

Materials:

1. (1) egg carton
2. scissors
3. tempera paint and brush
4. pipe cleaners
5. (1) 10″ x 10″ white tissue paper or paper doilies
6. (6) 1″ x 6″ green construction paper
7. ribbon or colored yarn

Steps:

1. Cut the egg carton cups into flower shapes.
2. Paint the flower shapes inside and out with tempera and let dry thoroughly.
3. Stick a pipe cleaner through the middle of the bottom for the stem, bending the top end over inside the cup.
4. Cut leaves from the green construction paper by folding the 1″ x 6″ strips and tapering the ends.

5. Fold the tissue paper in half one way and then in half the other way. Cut into a doily shape (rather like a snowflake). A pre-cut paper doily can be substituted.

6. Make a bouquet with the flowers and leaves and tape or tie together. Put the doily around and tie with the ribbon or yarn.

CRAYON AND WATERCOLORS

Materials:

1. black crayon
2. watercolor paints
3. paint brush
4. container with water
5. paper towel
6. (1) 9″ x 12″ white construction paper

Steps:

1. Draw an outline of a picture or design, using the black crayon and pressing very heavily.
2. Paint in the various parts of the picture with watercolor paints. (The crayon will keep the watercolors from running together.)

TISSUE GARDEN

Materials:

1. (4) 5″ x 5″ squares light green and yellow tissue paper
2. (2) 5″ x 5″ squares dark green tissue paper
3. (2) 5″ x 5″ dark colored tissue paper
4. (1) 9″ x 12″ white construction paper
5. container of liquid starch
6. scissors and paint brush

Steps:

1. Tear the light green and yellow tissue paper squares into small pieces, any shape.
2. Put a little starch on the white construction paper and put a piece of tissue down. Paint starch over it. Continue this until the paper is covered and pieces are over-lapping. This will make the background for the garden.

3. Cut one dark green square into ½″ strips for stems. Fold the other piece in quarters and then fold once more and cut out half a leaf shape. This will make 8 leaves.

4. Lay stems and leaves on the background while it is still wet. Lay some of the stems at angles so that the flowers will look like they are moving.

5. Cut out flowers all at the same time by folding both pieces of tissue together in quarters. Flowers can be any shape. Place flowers on stems and cover with starch

SPONGE FLOWERS

Materials:

1. (1) 9″ x 12″ construction paper for background, any color
2. pieces of torn sponge, each clipped with a clothespin
3. tempera paint: small amounts in egg cartons or muffin tins
4. construction paper for vase
5. scissors, black crayon

Steps:

1. Clip clothespins to the torn pieces of sponge. This will keep the paint off hands. Put small amounts of several colors of tempera paint, mixed with liquid starch, in egg cartons or muffin tins. Have a sponge for each color.

2. Dip sponge into paint, dab onto white paper, scattering various shapes of color over the top two thirds of the paper for flowers. Do the same for leaves. Let dry.

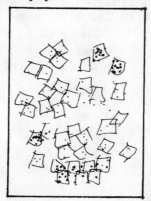

3. Cut a vase shape from construction paper. Paste onto drawing. Decorate with crayons.

4. Using black crayon, draw flower and leaf shapes on top of sponge painted shapes. Remind children that crayon shapes do not need to conform to the painted shapes.

CHALK ON BLACK PAPER

Materials:

1. (1) 9″ x 12″ or 12″ x 18″ black construction paper
2. container of liquid starch
3. bright colored chalk
4. newspapers

Steps:

1. Cover working surface with newspapers and put the chalk in small containers within easy reach.
2. Place the black construction paper in the middle of the newspaper. Pour about 3 tablespoons of liquid starch in the middle of the black paper. Smear all over the paper with the hand used for drawing. Make sure the edges are covered and the starch is evenly spread over the paper.

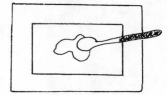
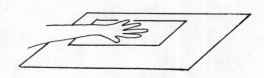

3. After spreading the starch on the paper, draw with the chalk. Work quickly, for when the starch dries it will be difficult to move the chalk over the paper. Any kind of design can be made. Try making large flowers, insects, fish or geometric shapes.
4. The starch will act as a fixative but to be sure the chalk does not rub off, spray the dry pictures with fixative or hair spray.

DROP AND BLOW PAINT

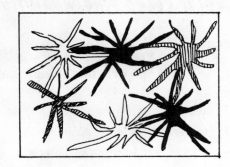

Materials:

1. 3 colors of thin tempera paint
2. a drinking straw
3. (1) 12" x 18" white construction paper

Steps:

1. Put two large drops of one color of tempera paint on the paper. Blow down on it with the straw. The paint will spread out. The paint can be controlled by turning the paper and blowing across in a particular direction. Let dry for a few minutes.

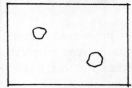 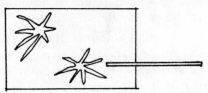

2. Put two or three large drops of a second color and repeat step one. The colors will overlap, but the first color should be dry enough so that the colors will not run.

 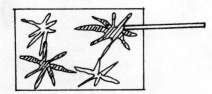

3. Repeat, using a third color.

 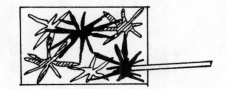

MULTI-COLOR FINGERPAINTING

Materials:

1. any size paper: fingerpaint paper, butcher or shelf paper
2. container of liquid starch
3. powdered tempera paint
4. newspapers and paper towels

Steps:

1. Place paper for fingerpainting on a piece of newspaper. Have a paper towel handy to wipe hands.
2. Pour 3 to 4 tablespoons of liquid starch in the middle of the paper and smear all over the paper. Be sure to get the edges.
3. Sprinkle small amounts of different colors of powdered tempera paint in various areas on the paper. Fingerpaint in the separate areas where the different colors were sprinkled. Blend the color edges together but do not rub over the whole paper or it will become a muddy color.

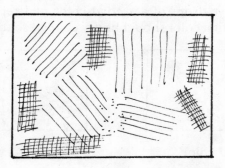

Suggestions:

—Very beautiful effects can be created by using two colors that will create a third color; yellow and blue; blue and red; yellow and red.
—Try using various shades of one color. Leave some white areas of the background paper showing through.
—These make beautiful covers for books or folders. To preserve, spray with clear plastic, lacquer or varnish.

STANDING ANIMAL

Materials:

1. (1) 9″ x 12″ colored construction paper
2. (1) 6″ x 9″ colored construction paper
3. pieces of yarn
4. scraps of construction paper for eyes, etc.
5. scissors and paste or glue

Steps:

1. Fold the 9″ x 12″ construction paper in half, lengthwise. Cut a half circle on the open edge. Cut one inch from each side on the center fold. Cut 1″ slits from each edge, toward the middle on the fold. Bend back to make the body stand.

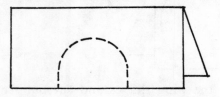
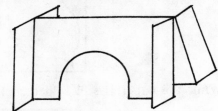

2. Cut out the animals face from the 6″ x 9″ piece of colored construction paper and facial features from the scraps. Paste onto the face.

3. Paste the head onto the folds of the legs at the top. Add yarn for hair, tail, etc.

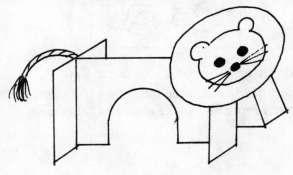

BUTTERFLY MOBILE

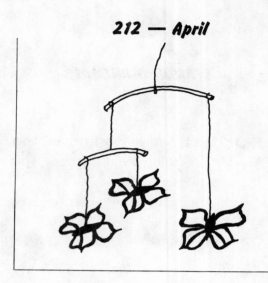

Materials:

1. black construction paper cut to various sizes (ex. 4½″ x 6″)
2. colored tissue paper
3. needle and thread
4. paste or glue
5. reeds, straws or stick to suspend butterflies.

Steps:

1. Fold two pieces of the black construction paper in half, widthwise. Cut out half of the shape of a butterfly. (You may wish to pencil this first.)

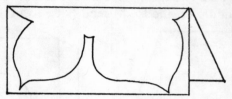

2. While the paper is still folded, cut into the wing shapes and cut out sections.

3. Unfold the shapes, paste on one side and lay on tissue paper. Put one shape on the other side of the tissue paper, back to back with the first so they match exactly.

4. When the paste is dry, trim the extra tissue paper away.
5. Using the needle and thread, attach the butterflies to the sticks. You can use just three butterflies or add more and make it more challenging.

SUN MOBILE

Materials:

1. (1) 9″ x 9″ square of yellow paper
2. scissors
3. needle and thread
4. pencil

Steps:

1. Draw a circle on the yellow construction paper, right to the edge of the paper. Draw a smaller circle in the middle. Draw a design around the outside edge of the circle. This can be any kind of design the child desires.

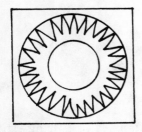 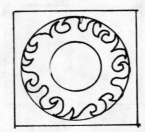 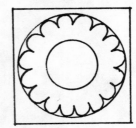

2. Cut out both circles and then cut the inside circle a bit smaller so it will swing in the middle.
3. Write or draw something on the center circle.
4. Sew the small circle into the middle of the sun.

Tie here and sew up to the top. Leave some string to hang the sun.

CARDBOARD LOOM WEAVING

Materials:

1. (1) 9″ x 12″ cardboard or chipboard
2. ruler or pencil
3. thin, strong string
4. scissors
5. yarn of all weights and colors

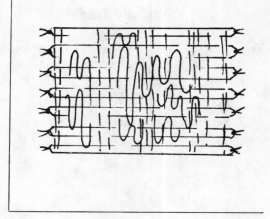

Steps:

1. Measure and mark a ½″ border on each 9″ edge of the 9″ x 12″ piece of cardboard or chipboard. Place a mark every ½″. Make slits on the half inch marks, ½″ deep along the 9″ border.

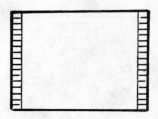

2. Tie a knot in one end of the string and slide under the first ½″ slit. Bring string across loom and slide through ½″ slit directly across. Loop under and slip up through the ½″ slit next to it. Continue to last slit and knot end of string.

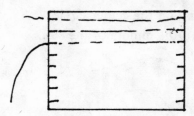

3. Weave in and out across the width of the loom with yarn of all colors and weights. Try making designs. Add ribbon and strips of fabric if desired.

4. To finish, cut the loops of string and tie two side-by-side strings together in a knot. Do this to all strings. This will remove the weaving from the loom so it can be used again.

COLLAGE PEOPLE

Materials:

1. (1) 9″ x 12″ construction paper of any color
2. (1) 6″ x 9″ pink construction paper
3. scraps of material for clothing
4. yarn for hair
5. odds and ends for decorating
6. scissors and paste or glue

Steps:

1. Fold the 6″ x 9″ pink construction paper lengthwise, and draw on half a body. Cut it out while the paper is still folded.

2. Paste the body onto the 9″ x 12″ construction paper but leave the arms and legs free so they can be bent into the position desired.

3. Cut clothes and shoes from materials and paste onto the body.
4. Ravel yarn for hair and paste on.
5. Add umbrellas, toys, flowers, etc.
6. Fold arms and legs into positions and paste down.

May

FLOWER BOUQUET

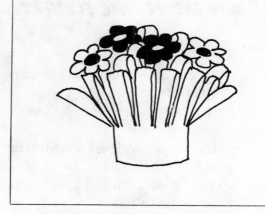

Materials:

1. (1) 9″ x 12″ green construction paper
2. (1) 9″ x 12″ colored construction paper
3. scraps of construction paper, all colors, for flowers
4. stapler
5. scissors and paste or glue

Steps:

1. Fold both 9″ x 12″ pieces of construction paper in half, lengthwise. Mark a line 1″ from the open edge across the width of the paper. Cut strips, about ½″ wide, from the folded edge up to the line.

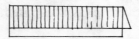

2. After cutting separate the two 9″ x 12″ pieces. Put paste or glue along one 12″ edge and paste about 1″ up from the other 12″ edge. Do this to both pieces. This will cause the strips to loop.

3. Roll the green piece with the staples to the inside and staple to hold the shape. This will cause the strips to stick out like leaves.

4. Roll the colored piece tighter and put it inside the green roll. You can staple this to the green.
5. Make all kinds of flowers with the scraps and paste them onto the ends of the colored strips in the center.

MAY BASKET WITH FLOWERS

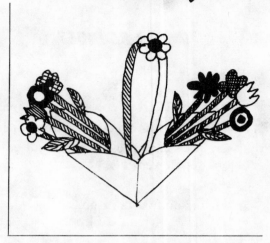

Materials:

1. (1) 9″ x 9″ colored construction paper (for basket)
2. (1) 1″ x 12″ same color construction paper as basket
3. (8-12) ½″ x 6″ green construction paper
4. scraps of all colors of construction paper to make flowers
5. scissors and paste or glue

Steps:

1. Fold the 2 opposite corner edges of the 9″ x 9″ colored construction paper to the center of the paper so they overlap, as illustrated.

2. Cut flowers and leaves from the construction paper scraps. Paste or glue them to the ½″ x 6″ strips of green paper. Paste or glue them to the inside of the basket as shown.

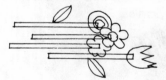 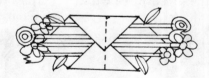

3. Fold the construction basket in half. Attach the 1″ x 12″ construction paper strip for a handle. Paste or glue the center parts of the basket together.

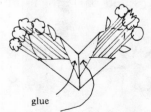 

glue

MAY BASKET

Materials:

1. (1) 9″x9″ piece of construction paper, any color
2. (1) 1″x9″ strip of construction paper for handle
3. liquid starch
4. metal container to make form over (coffee can is perfect)
5. rubber band

Steps:

1. Using hands, rub liquid starch all over both sides of the 9″x9″ piece of construction paper.
2. Drape the starch-covered piece of paper over the container, gathering so that it fits around. Secure with a rubber band.

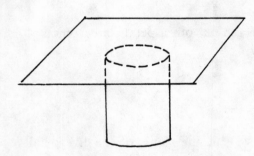

3. Remove gently, after snipping the rubber band with scissors. Glue on handle. Decorate, tie on ribbons and fill with flowers.

CREPE PAPER FLOWER

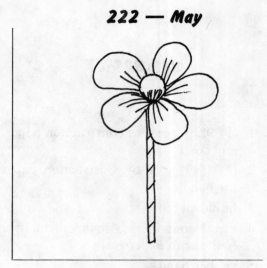

Materials:

1. (1) strip of green crepe paper 2 feet long
2. (5) 4″x4″ pieces of colored crepe paper
3. (1) 4″x4″ black crepe paper
4. (2) 3″ pieces of masking tape
5. straw
6. Kleenex

Steps:

1. Roll ½ of the Kleenex into a ball and wrap the 4″x4″ black piece of crepe paper around Kleenex ball and twist ends.

2. Fold the 5 pieces of crepe paper together and cut out a petal shape on the fold. Twist the bottom of each petal.

3. Tape the ball tail to the top of the straw. Put the stems of the five petals on the other piece of tape, next to each other. Tape it around the straw also, just next to the ball.

 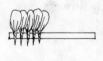

4. Stretch the green crepe paper strip and wrap the base of the flower and the straw. Begin at the base of the flower.

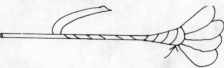

5. Puff out the flower petals to make the flower look nice.

TISSUE FLOWER

Materials:

1. (4) 9"x9" squares of tissue paper, each a different color
2. piece of string
3. scissors

Steps:

1. Stack the pieces of tissue paper on top of each other and fold together like a fan, accordian style.

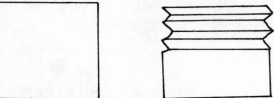

2. Fold in half, lengthwise, to find the middle. Tie a string around the middle, not too tightly. Do not gather. Round off the corners on each end of the fan.

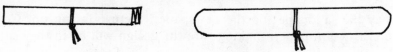

3. Spread out on each side of the middle, like an open fan. Carefully separate each layer of tissue paper, pulling gently to the center string.

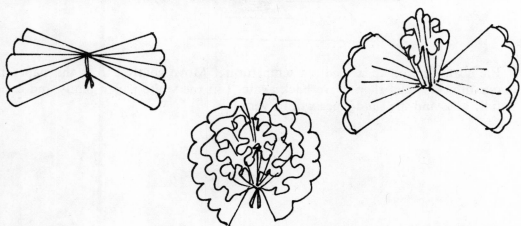

SANDPAPER PRINTS

Materials:

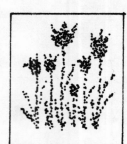

1. piece of fine grain sandpaper, any size
2. piece of white construction paper, twice the size of the sandpaper
3. crayons
4. iron and newspapers

Steps:

1. Draw a picture or design on the sandpaper. Color very heavily. Remind the children that if they use letters or words that they will come out backwards on the ironed print.

2. Lay the sandpaper on the newspaper, picture facing up. Cover with the white construction paper, making sure the design will be in the center.

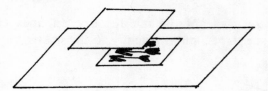

3. Pre-heat the iron to a medium temperature. Move gently across the paper in one direction and then move back again. Lift the white paper gently and carefully as it and the sandpaper will be very hot.

CIRCLE FLOWERS MOBILE

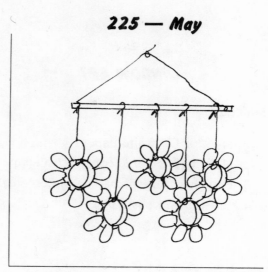

Materials:

1. (5) 1″ x 9″ strips of construction paper in pastel colors
2. (7-8) 1″ x 2″ pieces of construction paper in pastel colors for each flower (scraps of construction paper can be used)
3. (1) wire or wooden hanger
4. string or yarn
5. scissors and paste or glue

Steps:

1. Paste or glue the 1″ x 9″ construction paper strips into rings.

2. Trim the corners of the 1″ x 2″ pieces of construction paper to make petals as illustrated. Fold the straight edges at the bottom of the petals to make tabs.

3. Glue or paste the flower petal tabs to the paper rings at equal intervals.

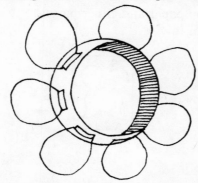

4. Tie one end of a piece of string to the flower and the other end to the hanger. Hang the flowers at different levels.

WINDOW ART

Materials:

1. (1) 9″ x 12″ white paper
2. (1) 9″ x 12″ colored construction paper
3. crayons, fingerpaints or watercolors
4. scissors and paste or glue

Steps:

1. On the piece of 9″x12″ white paper make an all-over design using either crayons, fingerpaints or watercolor paints. Stripes, repeat patterns, geometric shapes, lines or textures are a few that could be done.

2. Fold the 9″ x 12″ colored construction paper in half. On the folded edge cut half of a shape, design or figure. Save the outside edge.

3. Open up the construction paper and either paste or glue it to the top of the white paper with the design on it.

WATERCOLOR NEWSPAPER DESIGN

Materials:

1. watercolor paints
2. #7 or #10 paint brush
3. container of water and paper towels
4. a page of the classified section of the newspaper
5. (1) 12″ x 18″ black construction paper
6. scissors and paste or glue

Steps:

1. Spread out a section of the classified ads on the desk, making sure the columns are horizontal.

2. Paint in squares and rectangles in the columns of the paper, using many colors. Use the colors in the paint box and also try mixing other colors.

3. When dry, use a black crayon to outline the squares and rectangles of different colors. In each shape also make lines, circles, designs and textures.

4. To frame, fold the 12″ x 18″ black construction paper in half, widthwise, and mark a 1½″ border on the open edges. Cut out the center section. Paste the frame to the painted newspaper and trim away the extra paper.

YARN LINE DESIGNS

Materials:

1. (1) 6″ x 9″ or 9″ x 12″ tagboard or chipboard (cardboard boxes cut up also work well)
2. yarn, colored string, roving
3. white glue
4. scissors and pencil

Steps:

1. Using a pencil, lightly draw a picture on the heavy paper. Make sure that it is large and simple.

2. Put white glue along the lines of the picture and put yarn on top of the glue. Put glue inside the shapes and fill in with yarn. Fill in the background with a plain color of yarn.

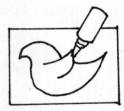  

3. You may wish to make the central shape a plain color and then use lots of different colors for the background. Remember when finished to check that all ends of yarn are glued down.

Variations:

—The following illustrations show other examples of designs instead of pictures, and combining fabric or colored paper with the yarn.

PAPER SCULPTURE

Materials:

1. (2) 9″ x 12″ pieces of construction paper of contrasting colors
2. white glue or paste
3. scissors
4. 5 or 6 paper clips

Steps:

1. Glue or paste 2 sheets of different colored construction paper together. Be sure to spread the glue or paste over the entire surface of the paper.

2. Cut the paper into various designs, making curved lines, straight strips, angular cuts, being careful not to make any completely through. The paper should have many cuts but still be in one piece. (Pencil lines can be made before cutting.)

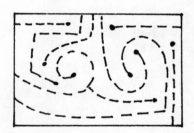

3. After cutting, bend and twist (gently) the strips into loops and attach with glue to another strip or section of paper. Look for interesting new shapes and color contrasts. Keep looping, twisting and attaching the strips until all loose ends are attached to other sections. (Use paper clips to hold attached strips until the glue sets.)

SHOE BOX PUPPET

Materials:

1. shoe box
2. a brown paper bag—#5
3. rubber band
4. paper and fabric scraps
5. tempera paint
6. scissors and paste or glue

Steps:

1. Use the bottom of the box for the front of the puppet's body. Cut a 2″ round hole in one end of the box for the puppet's paper bag neck. Paint the shoe box. See picture for ideas.

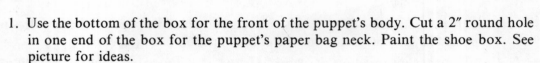

2. Stuff the brown paper bag half full of scraps or wrinkled newspaper and put a rubber band around the "neck".

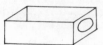

3. Cut slits up the paper bag "neck". Put the ends through the hole in the box and paste to the box.

4. Cut arms and legs from construction paper or fabric and paste to the box. Use crayons or tempera paint for facial features and yarn or roving for hair.

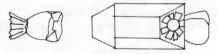

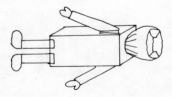

ME AND MY SHADOW

Materials:

1. (1) 4½" x 12" colored construction paper
2. (1) 4½" x 6" white construction or drawing paper
3. (1) 4½" x 6" black construction paper
4. crayons
5. scissors and paste

Steps:

1. Have each child draw and color an illustration of himself on the white paper. You might suggest that each one colors the figure in clothes such as he or she is wearing.

2. Place the white paper on top of the black construction paper and cut out the figure and the shadow figure at the same time. (You may wish to cut the figure first and then draw around it on the black and cut it separately.

3. Fold the colored construction paper in half. Paste the colored figure on one half with the feet at the fold. Place the black shadow on the other half with feet meeting feet.

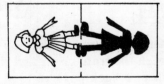

Hints:

1. Suggest that the children draw themselves at play.

2. They could draw themselves on larger paper, making the figures much bigger and do a mural.

3. Draw a picture of Mother at work for a Mother's Day card.

SQUEEZE PAINT BOOK COVER

Materials:

1. (1) 12″ x 18″ gray bogus paper or lightweight cardboard
2. tempera paint in plastic containers with squirt tops
3. (1) 3″ x 12″ colored construction paper
4. paint brush
5. scissors and glue

Steps:

1. Paint one side of the 12″ x 18″ gray bogus paper or lightweight cardboard with any color of tempera paint. Let dry.
2. Place the squirt bottles of paint on a table covered with newspaper.
3. To make designs squirt paint onto painted cardboard. Make various kinds of wavey lines and dribbles. Let dry throughly.

4. When dry, cut the cardboard in half, widthwise. Fold the 3″ x 12″ piece of construction paper in half, lengthwise and cover one side with glue. Bind the two pieces of painted cardboard together.

5. Pages can be stapled together and bound to the book with two strips of 2″ x 9″ paper. Paste each strip between the front cover and the first page and the second strip between the back cover and back page.

 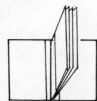

WAX PAPER TISSUE CUTOUTS

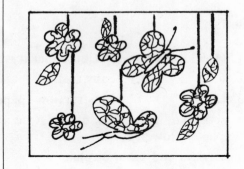

Materials:

1. two pieces of waxpaper, any size
2. tissue paper scraps
3. liquid starch in a small container
4. paint brush
5. scissors
6. paper punch and string

Steps:

1. Tear the tissue scraps into small pieces. Make a solid collage on the wax paper. First paint the wax paper with starch, lay on pieces of tissue and cover with starch. Be sure to cover completely with tissue and starch.

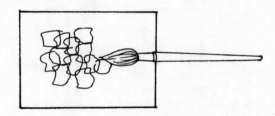

2. When the tissue and starch are completely dry, carefully peel away the wax paper. The tissue collage will stick together making one sheet of paper.

3. Cut shapes out of the tissue collage such as birds, flowers and butterflies.

4. Punch a hole in the top of each shape and tie a string through it. Use the string to hang the shapes in a window or a space where the light will show through the tissue collage.

MOTHER'S DAY CARD

Materials:

1. (1) 9" x 12" construction paper (card)
2. 6" x 9" green construction paper
3. (1) 4½" x 6" construction paper
4. scraps of all colors of construction paper (flowers)
5. scissors and paste or glue
6. pen, pencil or dark crayons

Steps:

1. Fold the 9" x 12" paper in half, widthwise for card.
2. Fold the 4½" x 6" construction paper for vase in half and cut out a vase. Put paste around the edges and paste onto the card, near the bottom.

 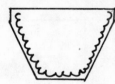

3. Cut out stems with leaves (or cut separately and add leaves) and make flowers to paste at the top. Have the child write on each stem the kind of chores which he will do for his mother. Slip flowers in vase.

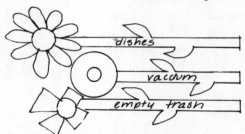 

4. Write poem on the pot or inside the card.

HAPPY MOTHER'S DAY

Pick a flower and
You will see
The jobs you'll pick
This week for me.

TISSUE OVER BOTTLES

Materials:

1. bottle, jar or tin can without any printing on it
2. liquid starch in small container
3. paint brush
4. shellac, varnish or clear plastic spray paint (optional)
5. tissue paper, many colors

Steps:

1. Tear or cut tissue paper into small shapes.
2. Apply pieces of tissue paper to chosen container, using the paint brush and liquid starch. Do a small area at a time. Put on some starch, pieces of tissue, and more starch on top of the tissue.

3. After it has dried, the entire surface can be sprayed with shellac, varnish or clear plastic.

Suggestions:

—If the containers have printing on them, first apply a coat of gesso or latex paint and let dry. It will not need as many coats of tissue and some of the background can be allowed to show through.

PAINT-GLUE RELIEF

Materials:

1. heavy paper such as tag, chip or card-board as in boxes
2. white glue in squeeze bottles
3. tempera paint and brushes
4. ink brayer
5. black printing ink or tempera paint
6. piece of wax paper, tinfoil or glass to put ink or paint on

Steps:

1. Using a pencil, lightly sketch in a design or picture on the heavy paper. Remember to keep it very simple; no small, tiny details.

2. Squeeze a fine line of glue straight from the bottle onto the pencil lines. Let the glue dry thoroughly.

3. Paint inside the picture or design with tempera paints. Keep the colors bright and thick. Cover all areas of the paper. Stay within the original lines and don't worry about the glue lines. If necessary, paint over them.

4. When the paint is dry, roll a brayer, covered with ink or black tempera paint, gently over the entire picture. Put a small amount of the ink or paint on the wax paper and roll the brayer over it. Before applying to the picture make sure the brayer does not have too much on it by testing on a piece of scratch paper.

CLOTH-WAX DESIGN

Materials:

1. (1) 6″x6″ piece of solid-color material
2. crayons
3. iron
4. (2) 6″x6″ pieces of white paper
5. tag board
6. yarn
7. glue

Steps:

1. Color a picture or design on the material. Color very heavy and dark.
2. Lay white paper down on a flat surface. On top of this place the cloth with the design facing up. Then put the other piece of white paper on top of the cloth. Iron with a very hot iron.

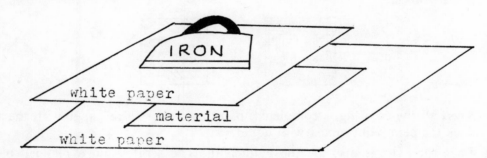

3. Glue the material to the tag board and paste on a piece of yarn for the hand, or make holes at the top to put the yarn through.
4. You can mount one of the white paper prints on colored construction paper for a picture.

CRAYON SCRATCH

Materials:

1. piece of lightweight cardboard or chipboard
2. old, peeled crayons
3. a sharp, pointed tool such as a toothpick, tapestry needle or something similar
4. newspapers
5. thick black tempera paint mixed with liquid soap and a paint brush

Steps:

1. Put newspaper to protect desk from crayon scraps.
2. Color the whole surface of the lightweight cardboard or chipboard with many colors. Press firmly, making the colors bright and solid. Color squares, circles or wavy lines.

3. When all the coloring is completed, paint over the entire paper with the thick black tempera paint mixed with liquid soap.
4. When the paint is dry, use the pointed tools to scratch out a planned picture or design. Create texture by using many shapes and design.

Hints:

—Remember to keep the paper in the middle of a piece of newspaper so the crayon scraps and paint chips will not go on the floor or this could be a very messy project.

STAR SPANGLED BANNER

Materials:

1. (1) white construction paper or butcher paper, any size
2. crayons
3. thin black tempera paint
4. paint brush
5. newspaper

Steps:

1. Draw a patriotic picture on the white paper with crayons. Color very heavily. Use bright colors.

2. Place drawing on newspaper.
3. Paint a coat of thin black, tempera paint over the entire picture. The wax drawing will show through the black paint.

PATRIOTIC PEOPLE MOBILE

Materials:

1. (2) 3″ x 3″ skin color construction paper
2. (2) 4″ x 6″ construction paper, any color for pants
3. (1) 3″ x 4″ construction paper, any color for shirt
4. scraps of construction paper: skin color, black, brown, red, white and blue
5. toothpick and (1) 18″ string
6. scissors and paste or glue

Steps:

1. Fold the two 3″ x 3″ pieces of skin color construction paper in half and trim off the open corners to make two heads.

2. Fold the two pieces of 4″ x 6″ construction paper in half, lengthwise and cut trousers. Fold the two 3″ x 4″ pieces of construction paper in half, widthwise, and cut two shirts. By cutting together they will be exactly the same.

3. Use scraps to make hands, feet, shoes, hair, a flag and anything else desired. Add details such as facial features and hair.

4. Lay one head, one shirt, one pair of trousers in a row. Paste or glue on the arms, feet, and shoes. Put glue or paste down the center of each piece and lay the 18″ piece of string down the middle, with all the extra string at the top. Put the other pieces on top.

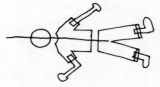 

PATRIOTIC TORCH

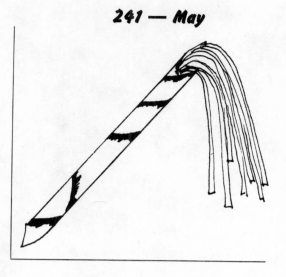

Materials:

1. (1) 12" x 9" grey bogus paper
2. red crayon
3. ½" strips of red, white and blue crepe paper (18" long)
4. stapler
5. paste or glue

Steps:

1. Color the edge of the bogus paper with the red crayon.

2. Gather about 6 of each color of crepe paper strips together and staple to the corner of the bogus paper.

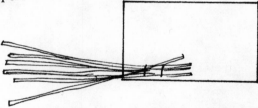

3. Roll the bogus paper from corner to corner, starting at the corner where the crepe paper is stapled. Roll so that the red edge shows.

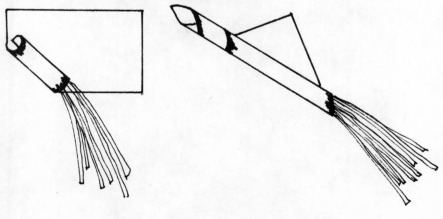

June

243

FROG PUPPET

Materials:

1. (1) 9" x 12" green construction paper
2. (2) 6" x 6" green construction paper
3. (1) 6" x 6" lime green construction paper
4. (2) 3" x 3" white construction paper
5. (2) 1½" x 1½" black construction paper
6. scissors and paste

Steps:

1. Put paste along one 9" edge of the 9" x 12" green paper and roll into a tube. Put paste on the inside of the tube about 2" down and pinch the top together. Round off the corners.

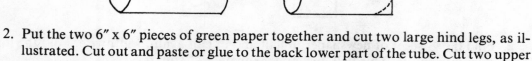

2. Put the two 6" x 6" pieces of green paper together and cut two large hind legs, as illustrated. Cut out and paste or glue to the back lower part of the tube. Cut two upper arms from the scraps and paste to the back of the tube.

3. Fold the two 3" x 3" white squares and the two 2" x 2" black squares in half and cut off the open corners for circles. Paste or glue the black circles to the upper part of the white circles.

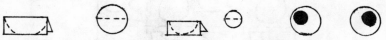

4. Fold the 6" x 6" lime green paper in half, lengthwise, and cut off the open corners to make the chest. Paste or glue chest and eyes to the tube. Add a mouth cut from black scraps.

REPEAT DESIGN

Materials:

1. (2) 4″ x 4″ pieces of gray bogus paper
2. ½ sheet newspaper, classified section
3. scissors, pencil or crayon
4. watercolors or tempera paint on pal-atte (wax paper stapled to a piece of cardboard)
5. soft bristle brush
6. container of water and paper towels

Steps:

1. Using the pencil draw a different shape on each piece of gray bogus. Cut out.

2. Fold the ½ sheet of newspaper in half and in half again, widthwise. Fold the long strip into thirds. This will give approximately 4″ squares.

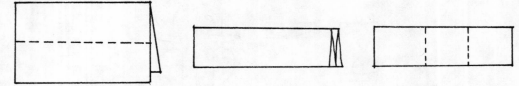

3. Open the newspaper and lay flat on desk. Using the shapes from gray bogus, create a repeat pattern in the 4″ squares. The shapes can be in the squares, on the fold lines, overlap etc.

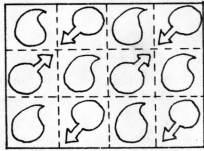

4. Use the paint to link the shapes together by means of painted lines, spaces, etc. Textures can be added to give variety. Remind the children to let some of the newspaper show through and be a part of the design.

OCEAN RESIST

Materials:

1. (1) 12" x 18" white paper
2. crayons
3. blue and green tempera paint (very, very thin) or water color paints
4. paint brush, wide bristle
5. container of water

Steps:

1. Draw and color an underwater ocean scene with all the sea life you can think of. Be sure to color very dark.

2. Paint over the picture with alternate lines of green and blue paint. Make sure the paint is very thin and that you do not go over the picture too many times. If you do, this will break down the crayon wax resist.

blue

green

blue

green

FINGERPAINT OCEAN SCENE

Materials:

1. (1) 12″ x 18″ white paper
2. blue and green powdered tempera paint
3. container of liquid starch
4. crayons

Steps:

1. Using the crayons, draw an ocean scene on the 12″ x 18″ white paper. Color heavily, use bright colors and fill the whole paper.

2. When the drawing is completed, place on a piece of newspaper. Pour on 2 to 3 tablespoons of liquid starch and smear all over the picture, making sure to get the edges.

3. Sprinkle green and blue powdered tempera paints in various sections over the picture. Mix the paint with the starch. Do a fingerpainting over the top of the drawing. Work fairly rapidly so the wax resistance is not broken.

FISH DESIGN

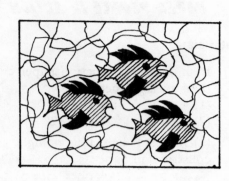

Materials:

1. 5″ x 5″ squares of tissue paper: light blue and green for background bright colors for fish
2. small container of liquid starch
3. (1) 9″ x 12″ white or light blue construction paper
4. paint brush and scissors

Steps:

1. Tear the 5″ x 5″ squares of light blue and green tissue paper into small pieces.
2. Cut out several fish shapes from the bright colored tissue paper squares. Cut body from one color and the fins and eyes of another color.

3. Cover the 9″ x 12″ white or light blue construction paper with a coat of liquid starch. Lay the pieces of light blue and green tissue paper on and cover each piece with another layer of starch.

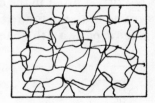

4. While the background is still wet place the fish where desired and paint starch over the top of them. Add seaweed made of dark green tissue if desired.
5. When dry the fish shapes can be outlined with black crayon and sea plants can be added with other crayons.

PAPER PEOPLE IN ACTION

Materials:

1. flesh color construction paper cut to these measurements:
   (1) 4″ x 3″   (1) 1″ x 8″
   (2) 2″ x 2″   (2) 1″ x 12″
2. (1) 12″ x 18″ light blue or light green construction paper
3. scraps of paper, fabric and yarn for buttons
4. scissors and paste or glue

Steps:

1. Fold the two 2″ x 2″ squares in half, together, and cut off the open corners to make circles. Fold the 3″ x 4″ piece of construction paper in half, lengthwise, and cut off the open corners. This will make the head, hips and chest.

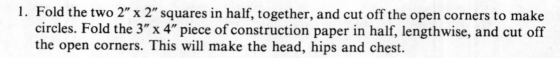

2. Fold the two 1″ x 12″ strips together in half and in half again widthwise. Cut into sections on the fold lines. Curve the corners off each piece. This will make the arms and legs.

3. Lay the parts of the body in the correct order in the center of the 12″ x 18″ construction paper. Move the parts around until the figure shows some type of action. Lift one piece at a time, apply glue or paste to the back and attach to the paper.

4. Using scraps of fabric, paper and yarn, cut clothes for the figures. Also add details such as hair, eyes, jump ropes, baseballs and bats.

FINGER PUPPETS

Materials:

1. cotton balls or kleenex
2. (1) 3″ x 3″ flesh or pink material
3. (1) 1½″ x 2½″ piece of fabric, plain or print
4. marking pens or crayons
5. scraps of yarn, lace, paper, fabric and buttons
6. scissors, glue and string

Steps:

1. Wrap the flesh or pink square of fabric over the cotton ball (or ½ a kleenex wadded up) and tie with string.

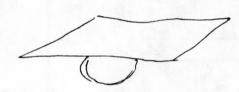   

2. Glue the 1½″ x 2½″ piece of fabric around the pink fabric where it is tied with string. Make sure it is tight enough to stay on the finger. This will cover the extra pink fabric and make the body of the puppet.

3. Decorate a face on the pink fabric with the marking pens or crayons. Use the yarn to make hair. Add details with the scraps of fabric, lace, ribbon and buttons. Glue these on.

AQUARIUM

Materials:

1. (1) shoe box
2. blue and black tempera paint
3. sand and sea shells
4. scraps of construction paper, all colors
5. thread or string
6. scissors and glue

Steps:

1. Paint the inside of the shoe box with the blue tempera paint and the outside of the box with black tempera paint. Let dry throughly.

2. Turn the shoe box on its side and put glue on what is to be the bottom of the aquarium. Sprinkle sand on the glue. Also glue on sea shells and anything else such as driftwood and dried weeds.

3. Use the scraps of construction paper to make fish. Cut two of each shape. Place a piece of string between the two matching shapes and glue together. Decorate the fish with scraps of paper and crayons.

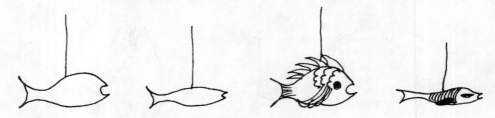

4. Hang the fish from the top of the inside of the box. Put a little white glue on the end of the string and press to the inside top of the box. (They can also be taped.) Make them hang at different lengths.

5. As an added effect, a piece of clear plastic or colored cellophane paper can be attached to cover the front of the aquarium.

WHALE MOBILE

Materials:

1. (1) 9″ x 12″ sheet of newsprint
2. (1) 9″ x 12″ piece of heavy black rail-board
3. (3) 1″ x 3″ scraps of colored construction paper
4. scissors
5. needle and thread

Steps:

1. Draw a whale shape on newsprint. Draw a hole in the middle. Cut out and use as a pattern.

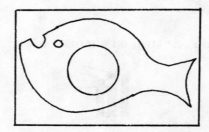

2. Trace around the newsprint pattern onto the black railboard and cut it out.
3. Cut three little fish from the scraps of construction paper.
4. String the little fish in a line with the needle and thread. Tie to the tip of the hole in the whale.

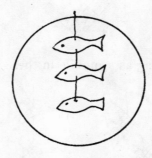

5. Tie a string to the top of the whale to hang it.

WOVEN FISH

Materials:

1. (6) 1″ x 12″ strips of colored construction paper (2 colors)
2. scissors and glue or paste
3. string

Steps:

1. Fold the strips of construction paper in half. Interlock two pieces as shown and paste or glue into place.

2. Weave three strips onto one strip on alternate edges. Secure with paste or glue.

3. Weave in the cross strips, first one side and then the other. Secure all strips in place with glue. Cut as shown.

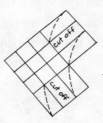

4. The folded fish can be hung as a mobile in these ways:

SPRING-TISSUE MOBILE

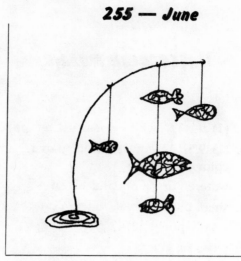

Materials:

1. scraps of tissue paper
2. wax paper
3. glue mixture, (½glue, ½water)
4. paint brush and scissors
5. a coat hanger and string or thread
6. lump of clay
7. newspapers

Steps:

1. Lay newspaper on the desk. Pour some of the glue mixture into a small container.

2. Cut two pieces of wax paper the same size. Lay on the newspaper. Using the paint brush, cover one piece of the wax paper with glue. Lay on pieces of tissue paper. Cover completely with glue mixture.

3. Dip a piece of string in the glue, coat with glue and then lay on the tissue-covered wax paper in a shade wished. Be sure the two ends of the string meet. Then lay the other piece of wax paper on top and press down. Hold until it sticks firmly.

4. When this is dry, trim around the design right next to the string.

5. After trimming, use string or a needle and thread to string each shape.

6. Untwist the coat hanger and bend into a slight curve. You may wish to cut one end off so it won't be too long. Then place one end of the wire in a lump of clay to anchor it.

7. When the clay is dry, tie the shapes onto the hanger. You may want to secure the strings to the wire with a bit of glue.

Variations:

—You may wish to hang the folded fish in the weaving section.

—Perhaps you would like to hang the single string mobiles or puppets from this wire.

WATERCOLOR MOSAIC

Materials:

1. (1) 9"x12" white construction paper
2. (1) 9"x12" construction paper, any color
3. watercolor paints and brush
4. small container of water
5. small sponge, 2"x2"
6. paste or glue

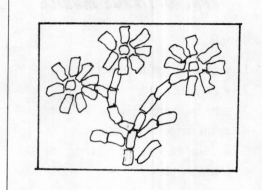

Steps:

1. Dip sponge in water and make one side of the paper wet. Turn over and stretch tightly on the desk so there are no wrinkles. Make the top side wet.

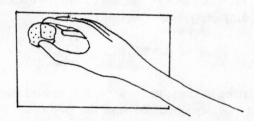

2. Paint bright colored stripes across the width of the paper with the watercolor paints.

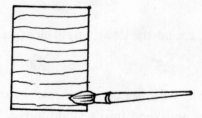

3. When the painting is dry, tear into small pieces. Arange on the 9" x 12" piece of colored construction paper to create any kind of design or picture. When the pieces are in positions desired, lift one at a time, apply paste or glue and replace on the paper.

YARN ANIMALS

Materials:

1. (1) 12″ x 18″ construction paper, any color
2. roving or thick yarn, many colors
3. scissors and paste or glue
4. pencil

Steps:

1. Draw the outline of an animal on the 12″ x 18″ construction paper. Keep it large and simple.

2. Squeeze glue on the outline and press on the appropriate color of yarn around the outline.

3. Cut roving or yarn into small pieces and pull these pieces with fingers to make fuzz. Glue on the animals body for fur.

4. Add eyes, nose, tongue, etc., with other colors or yarn.

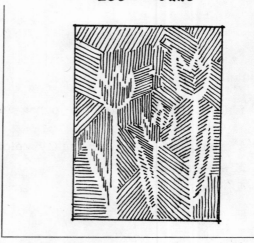

CHALK OVER WHITE GLUE

Materials:

1. white glue in a squeeze bottle
2. (1) 9″ x 12″ white construction paper or light-weight tagboard
3. colored chalk
4. a pencil
5. piece of kleenex or cotton

Steps:

1. Draw a design or picture on the white paper with a pencil. Squeeze white glue on all the pencil lines, fairly thick. Let this dry thoroughly.

2. Smear or smudge different colors of chalk over the picture or design with finger-tips, piece of kleenex or cotton. The white glue will resist the chalk, showing through clear and white. This technique creates a misty, delicate picture.

CHALK LANDSCAPES

Materials:

1. (1) 9″ x 12″ newsprint
2. (1) 9″ x 12″ white construction paper
3. colored chalk
4. newspaper

Steps:

1. Place the 9″ x 12″ newsprint on top of the 9″ x 12″ white construction paper. Hold the top of the two pieces of paper with one hand and with the other hand, tear a 1″ strip the width of the bottom of the newsprint.

2. Using a shade of green chalk, rub the side of the chalk down over the torn edge of the newsprint onto the white paper. Smudge the chalk on the white paper with fingertips or cotton for a misty effect.

3. Tear another strip from the bottom of the newsprint and repeat step #2 with another shade of green chalk.

4. Continue, repeating these steps all the way to the top of the white paper. Use various colors of chalk to create hills, mountains, sky, clouds.
5. When the background is complete, draw on trees, houses or anything else desired in the foreground with chalk.

Suggestions:

—Create a desert scene using light brown paper and shades of yellow, orange and brown chalk.

NIGHT CITIES

Materials:

1. (1) 9″ x 12″ black construction paper
2. crayons or chalk, bright colors
3. scissors

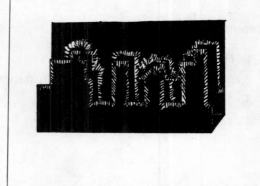

Steps:

1. Fold the 9″ x 12″ black construction paper in half, lengthwise. Open and make another fold, about 1½″ from center fold. This will create a 3-D effect; one section lower than the other and standing out.

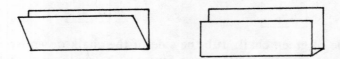

2. On the lower section, sketch a row of city buildings or houses. Cut out. Do not cut closer than 1″ from the fold.

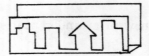   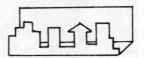

3. Fold the cities flat against the back, taller section. Using the bright colored crayons or chalk, go around each building shape with short, heavy strikes or lines. This will create the effect of night lights.

FATHER'S DAY CARD

Materials:

1. (1) 4″ x 12″ colored construction paper, for card
2. scraps of construction paper, all colors
3. scissors and paste or glue
4. crayons

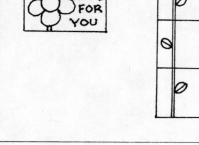

Steps:

1. Fold the 4″ x 12″ paper in half twice, widthwise, until you have a 3″ x 4″ package.

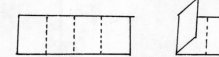

2. Make a flower on the front section with a stem. Put on writing.

3. Open and make a flower with a stem on the first section. Open again and add another stem and leaf. Repeat in each section to the last.

 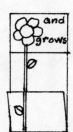 

Index